Praise for THE VISITOR:

"*The Visitor* is the best book I have found on creating great customer service in the church. An easy read and a must in training leadership and ministry teams on how to create an atmosphere where the first time visitor keeps coming back. A must read!"

~Chantell M. Cooley,
Vice-President of Columbia Southern University

"*The Visitor* book should be on every pastor's and church staff member's 'must read list.' The use of the Queen of Sheba's visit to King Solomon's house and temple, and his comparison and practical application of that to modern day visitors to the church, is sheer genius—no, more than that—it is truly inspired! Learn and apply these priceless principles of reaching and keeping visitors to your church. You'll be glad you did!"

~Howard Beam, serving 45 years in Pastoral Ministry,
Oversees Shepherds Rest, a ministry to pastors and missionaries

"I am pleased to recommend *The Visitor* to you and your teams. Pastor Lee has done an excellent job wrapping the importance of receiving visitors and the elements of doing so in a package that is not only highly readable and practical, but keeps the main thing the main thing that is the spiritual implications and impact that we all desire to see occur when people honor us with a visit."

~Buford Lipscomb,
Sr. Pastor Liberty Church,
President Liberty Network International

"In a church world marked by mediocrity and a "that's good enough" attitude, this book is just in time. It will inspire and equip every church leader with the tools they need to reveal Gods glory within the context of their own ministry. When it's over, visitors will step through your doors and have their breath taken away."

~JP Wilson,
Pastor Liberty Church

THE VISITOR

EXCEEDING EXPECTATIONS TO
IMPACT THE FIRST TIME VISITOR

LEE WEST

bush
PUBLISHING
& associates

The Visitor
ISBN: 978-0-9836109-2-2
Copyright © 2014 Lee West
www.LeeWest.org

Bush Publishing & Associates books may be ordered at www.bushpublishing.com or www.amazon.com.

For further information, please contact:
Bush Publishing & Associates
www.bushpublishing.com

DEDICATION

This book is dedicated to my wife Missy whom
I love with all my heart.

Table of Contents

INTRODUCTION

Are you ready to turn unbelieving, skeptical, first time visitors into believing, regular attenders fulfilling the purpose and plan of God for their lives? Throughout this book, there is a weaving of the story thread from the Queen of Sheba's visit to the kingdom of Solomon. It examines how his ministry teams were the difference in the way the Queen entered the kingdom and the way she left the kingdom.

Every community is filled with queen of Shebas who are unbelieving and skeptical about what they have heard about the Kingdom. The church has touted, rightly so, that the Kingdom of God is the most desirable place to be, and how ones life can be changed dramatically by entering it here on earth. Sunday messages, billboards, newspaper columns, flyers, etc… have been broadcasted to our communities about how awesome God and His Kingdom are. We do this in order to get the skeptical unbeliever to become a visitor to our church. The issue has never been with our message or the methodology in which we delivered it, but has been in how we confirm our message as the visitor finally decides to walk through our front door for the very first time. You generally have 7-10 minutes to either make someone feel welcomed (not greeted) and accepted (not cliquish), or to confirm their skepticism that they have felt all along. The message that we broadcast to the world about Jesus is truly a miracle message, and one that is remarkably difficult for some to believe. It will be up to your ministry teams to confirm the message of love, care, and acceptance, not the preaching. The Queen of Sheba was changed, and left a different person than she came in because of the way Solomon's ministry teams served her, not by Solomon's message. Are we really ready to change our communities? Are we ready to spend as much effort in our preparation as we do in our presentation? Are we ready to close the back door so often referred to those that visit, swirl around, and then leave to go somewhere else, in order to achieve sustainable growth? The message in this book will offer some insight and guidelines to help with these efforts. One of my favorite passages of scripture tells me that the horse is prepared for battle, but the victory is from the Lord. God wants to work with us for victory, and one of the truest victories a church can obtain is turning an unbelieving, skeptical, first time visitor into a believing, faith filled, regular attender serving the purpose and plan of God for their life. If we are willing to take a hard look at our ministry teams as the catalyst for changing a community, and willing to execute the change among our teams, nothing is impossible.

*Could it be
that we have
concentrated
so much on the
spirit of man, that
we have left the
soul of man
wanting?*

CHAPTER ONE

SOLOMON AND THE QUEEN

There is a fascinating story in the bible that we have most likely read many times. It is a story that reveals the hearts of a king and a queen, a lot of wealth, a conquest for knowledge, and a display of wisdom unsurpassed by any other. In the midst of this story is also a subtle truth that penetrates right to the core of our existence, to our desires, to our emotions, and to our culture.

This subtle truth begins with one word buried right in the middle of I Kings 10:1-7. One word found in verse 4 where the queen reveals that wisdom can be "seen", and its this visual wisdom of excellence that makes a believer out of an unbelieving first time visitor to the kingdom. The word "seen" reveals that wisdom is not just heard, but is capable of being viewed, and what we see can change what we believe.

The story is found in I Kings 10:1-7 and discloses the visit of a very wealthy Queen of Sheba who has heard in her own land about King Solomon, a king who is supposed to have an unprecedented amount of wealth and wisdom. This unbelievable report has created a burning desire in her heart to know more and to articulate a visit to the king to see if the elaborate reports that she has heard are indeed true.

I Kings 10:1-7 (NKJV)

Now when the queen of Sheba heard of the fame of Solomon concerning the name of the Lord, she came to test him with hard questions. 2 She came to Jerusalem with a very great retinue, with camels that bore spices, very much gold, and precious stones; and when she came to Solomon, she spoke with him about all that was in her heart. 3 So Solomon answered all her questions; there was nothing so difficult for the king that he could not explain it to her. 4 And when the queen of Sheba had seen all the wisdom of Solomon, the house that he had built, 5 the food on his table, the seating of his servants, the service of his waiters and their apparel, his cupbearers, and his entryway by which he went up to the house of the Lord, there was no more spirit in her. 6 Then she said to the king: "It was a true report which I heard in my own land about your words and your wisdom. 7 However I did not believe the words until I came and saw with my own eyes; and indeed the half was not told me. Your wisdom and prosperity exceed the fame of which I heard.

So one day King Solomon has a visitor; a skeptical, unbelieving queen, known as the Queen of Sheba. To her surprise she finds that what she had heard was not even half of what she is seeing. King Solomon had exceeded the expectations of a first time visitor to his kingdom. He had exceeded her expectations so much that she makes a statement that we have read over and over as we have read this story, but may not have truly captured the essence of her experience. Verse 4 states that the Queen of Sheba had "seen" the wisdom of Solomon. It is very rare to see wisdom; in fact I don't believe I have ever heard anyone refer to wisdom as something you can visually see. Many times we hear references to hearing wisdom, but never to seeing wisdom.

What was it that made this very wealthy, skeptical queen reveal something so captivating as being able to see wisdom? This passage continues on to say in verse 7 that she was also unbelieving. She had heard about the fame, the magnificence, the enormous wealth, and the wisdom, but she didn't believe it. The Queen of Sheba is very similar to those that come through the front doors of our church. She was an unbelieving, skeptical first time visitor. She had heard so many great things about this kingdom, but had never experienced it. It was supposed to be a kingdom in which the king and ruler-ship was wise, had wealth beyond measure to care for those in the kingdom, and obtained peace from their enemies. It was also a kingdom that was filled with a community of happy servants.

The Queen of Sheba sounds similar to the churches target audience, and whom Jesus commissioned us to reach out to. Do you have a Queen of Sheba in your community? Do you have a skeptical person in your community that has heard all the wonderful things about the Kingdom of God but doesn't believe it? Our communities are filled with people that have heard all about how great the Kingdom of God is and how they should be a part of it. We have broadcasted for years that if you come to the Lord and come to our church, all your needs will be met, or at least most of your needs. We have told them they will have wise rulers, overseers, or pastors to speak into their life, financial increase will come due to tithing, peace will overtake their life, and a community awaits them to love them, care for them, and help them be a happy servant. Sounds a little like Solomon's kingdom.

The issue is not the message, but the realization of the message. Matthew chapter 6 even tells us to seek first the kingdom of God and all these things will be added unto you. It is God's plan and will for you to be taken care of. The bible lays out a very clear path for us to follow that unveils a plan for God to completely meet every one of our needs. For the church, we have never really been able to deliver on the promises that we have made. We struggle each week to retain first time visitors who are seeking that which they have heard. What they have heard unfortunately is not what we have been accurately able to deliver; therefore instead of making believers out of unbelievers we have confirmed their skepticism.

Do you remember a first time visit to a church? How did you feel? What were the thoughts going through your mind as you were preparing to walk out of your home to attend this unknown church? Were you nervous, wanting to come in late so you can slip in the back unnoticed to spy out the land? I think we all know there is a lot of concern with first time visits. Somewhere in the heart of a first time visitor they have to muster enough faith to walk through those doors hoping that what they have heard will actually be a reality. They have heard about this loving God and that Christians are supposed to be friendly, welcoming and loving. Unfortunately many stories have resulted from disastrous first time visits that had no resemblance of God, love or friendliness.

A few years back we were renting a facility for our weekend church service. Two ladies had showed up one Sunday morning to worship with us. They were first time visitors. The way our facility is laid out the restrooms are very obvious in the lobby area and are usually a safe lily pad to jump onto after entering as a first time guest. It's a good place to catch your breath before making the trek to our sanctuary. The two ladies made their way to the restroom only to find that it was not very clean. Our children's pastor overheard their conversation of disgust, and they made the dreaded comment that they will never come back to this church ever again. We lost the opportunity that morning to minister to these two ladies. As far as we know they have never returned.

Some time ago I was watching a documentary about the McDonalds Corporation and what had made them so successful. During an interview on the documentary with the manager of the largest McDonalds store in America a challenging question was poised. The question was simply, "What is the number one reason why your store is so successful?" The manager didn't have to think about it at all, and responded that the reason was clean restrooms. Clean restrooms were the reason why the top McDonalds restaurant in America was so successful. It's amazing that the things we think are the big bang for the buck are not always the case. It's the things we miss; that we overlook as important, that can produce the greatest results.

In regards to those two ladies that came to visit our church we could look at that as immature, silly, and not a very spiritual way of making a decision about church, but it's the reality we live in. We have to minister to people's souls to earn the right to minister to their spirit. Their soul deals with how they feel and we didn't do such a good job in making them feel loved. We provided dirty restrooms for them and that was the first impression we offered. Our vision statement here at our church simply states that we are, "An Oasis of Love and Hope in a World of Darkness and Hurt". Unfortunately that day, the day it counted the most, the oasis was pretty dry. Our words, that we so elegantly marketed to the world was not what we delivered. In fact, it was not even close.

The Queen of Sheba said that she saw wisdom. The fact is, wisdom can be seen. This passage is revelatory to the fact that wisdom is not only heard, but is open to the visual sense. Do first time visitors to your church see your wisdom? If not, what do they see? It may take some thought and effort, but it's possible to show wisdom, and the experience of the queen helps us to understand the intrinsic value of visual wisdom. As we read this passage it helps us to see the areas where wisdom transformed from something heard to something seen. Solomon's wisdom was seen in the details. It was the small things that produced the greatest impact. It's in the small things that provide the greatest opportunities. You will have to train yourself to think small to achieve the big things hoped for.

As we look closer at verse 4 of this passage, we see some very practical and revealing things that Solomon had put into play that created a great first impression, and that exceeded the queen's expectations. The queen says that she had seen all the wisdom of Solomon, the house that he had built, the food that was displayed on his table, the way or process that his servants went about their seating, the way that his waiters or his ministers served the people, the way his cupbearers served, and the way of his entrance. After watching this display of serving she said that she had no more spirit in her. The way that Solomon's ministry teams served actually took the Queen of Sheba's breath away. She experienced a moment where everything became very still, a hush in her spirit where refreshing takes place, a moment that would forever change her view of this kingdom, a moment that changed her life. It was the moment where she became a believer.

Have we thought about our ministry teams and the way they serve to the point that shows the wisdom of God? What are the small things that we can do as we serve to take the breath away from people? What can we do as a church that will make people stand or sit in awe? Could it be that we have concentrated so much on the spirit of man, that we have left the soul of man wanting? Have we alienated in our churches the very part of the human existence that feels? Have we missed the opportunities to share the gospel message because we really didn't care about the person's emotions? Have we traded our focus on the destination of the person at the expense of the person? We have all heard that people don't care how much you know until they know how much you care, but have we truly implemented this statement into our church culture, or is it just a cool phrase to say.

Proverbs 4 says that wisdom is the principal thing. Principal means it is the most important. Merriam Webster's dictionary gives a few examples on the definition of the word principal. One of the examples says that, "Vegetables are the principal ingredients in this soup." The other says, She is the principal cellist of the orchestra." Without vegetables in vegetable soup what would the soup look like? If the cellist were the principal musician of the orchestra, what would the orchestra sound like without the cellist? If wisdom is the principal thing in serving, then what does serving look like without wisdom? It's a scary thought to know that we might be serving up vegetable soup with no vegetables, or marketing our cellist orchestra with no cellist.

Do we seek wisdom as the principal thing and not forget, forsake or turn away from it as commanded in Proverbs chapter 4? Do we seek it as treasure or value it more precious than silver or gold? Do we make it our number one pursuit? Solomon had an understanding of wisdom and he took that understanding and imparted it into those that served under his leadership. For every ministry team that Solomon had under his charge, to be all on the same page representing him and revealing wisdom, it would appear that an impartation would have had to occur. It was an impartation of wisdom into his ministry teams. Kind of like a DNA transfer. Solomon understood that you could reveal the wisdom of the kingdom by the way you served. It's an important lesson for us to know that we too can reveal the wisdom of the Kingdom (God's Kingdom) by the way our ministry teams serve. Remember, that the Kingdom of God is within you, and where you go the Kingdom goes. We can reveal all the great and wonderful things of God to those around us, or we can allow this power to lay dormant. We have to be careful in our serving since we are on display to the world. Unfortunately, the lack of wisdom is also clearly seen and can become a visual thorn in our side, instead of a visual display of God's love for a hurting world.

The good news is that wisdom is readily available to us and is actually crying out to us. Proverbs 8 reveals the cry of wisdom and shows us that wisdom wants to be found and positions herself out in the open as to not be missed.

Proverbs 8:1-6 (NKJV)

Does not wisdom cry out, and understanding lift up her voice? 2 She takes her stand on the top of the high hill, beside the way, where the paths meet. 3 She cries out by the gates, at the entry of the city, at the entrance of the doors: 4 To you, O men, I call, and my voice is to the sons of men. 5 O you simple ones, understand prudence, and you fools, be of an understanding heart. 6 Listen, for I will speak of excellent things, and from the opening of my lips will come right things;

Wisdom is in the most visible places. It's on the high hill where everyone can see it. It's where the paths meet, which is where the most people will be found. It's at the gates or the entrances to the city. It's at the entrance of the doors. Wisdom has positioned herself to be found, uninhibited, unbound, open to all, free to be received and is crying out to mankind. What is the cry of wisdom? Verse 6 states that wisdom is speaking of excellent things, the things that are right. I don't know about you, but I want to do the things that are right. I want to know right, do right, be right, and serve right. The opposite of right is wrong. I don't want to know wrong, do wrong, be wrong, or serve wrong. Wisdom is crying out excellence to all mankind from the high hill and telling us how to serve right. Wisdom, with tears, is clearly revealing that she wants to be seen and heard, and similarly we have a hurting world, with tears, that is crying out to be seen and heard. Everyone has a story to tell, and as the two ladies that never returned to our church, unfortunately, we will never get to hear theirs.

With all the social media available and used by Americans some still have labeled us the loneliest country in the world. We have traded relational availability for connectivity. Our social media profiles say that we have hundreds of friends but in reality we cant share our deepest hurts with any of them. The world is searching for something to love them, something that will accept them, something that will offer them a hope and a future. The church is the catalyst that can provide the hope for our hurting world. Many people believe that the only way for the church to reach their communities is through a mighty move of God. So they wait and pray for God to move in their communities. I think God is waiting for a mighty move of man. We can't pray for God to give us more, if we are not willing to utilize what He has already given us. He has laid out the groundwork for us and gave us the Great Commission, gave us power and authority, and charged us to go and do as He did. We are to make disciples, and to make disciples we have to reach people, and people are attracted to excellence.

Have you ever wondered why deep within the heart of mankind there is a longing for excellence? Why does someone exceeding our expectations captivate us? If cost were not an issue we would stay in a 5 star hotel rather than a one star hotel, or eat at a 5 star restaurant rather than a 1 star. Have we really ever asked ourselves why we feel this way? Sure we can spell out the obvious like it's just nicer, or the beds are more comfortable and surface elements such as those, but why are we attracted to those elements? What is it in us that longs to be treated with excellence?

This innate characteristic of the human nature for excellence cannot be turned on and off, nor can it be compartmentalized when entering different establishments. Every day, 24 hours a day, 7 days a week we long for excellence. I have never met a person regardless of economic status, race, sex, religious affiliation, time of day or year, that didn't choose the 5 star hotel over the 1 star when asked and no cost was involved. Our desire for excellence is always on.

This is true no matter if you walk into a Nike store, Starbucks, Ice Cream Shop, Barnes & Nobles, Old Navy, Saks Fifth Avenue, or even the Church. It is my desire that Solomon's Inspiration can help the church and the church's ministry teams understand the importance of excellence and exceeding expectations through our serving. It made a believer out of the Queen of Sheba, and it will make a believer out of your visitors as well.

What is also challenging in the Proverbs 8:1-6 is that, like wisdom, most of our ministry teams are in the most visible places. They are seen in the places at the entrances and where the paths of the people meet. They are visible to all and are like the high places. If our ministry teams are so visible, maybe we should take more care into how they serve and what they are visually crying out as the people walk by. If you looked at your greeting team from a distance what would you see? What about your ushers or maybe your children's check in process? What would these teams reveal to you? Would they reveal wisdom? Have you observed their serving? Are they confirming that your mission or vision statement is true, or are they revealing a work in progress? Our systems and processes can be a work in progress, but our vision statement cannot be. We have to deliver upon what we are broadcasting to the community or otherwise we confirm their skepticism. If you have a billboard that advertises your church as a place of love and hope, then your people should provide love and hope. They will never find love and hope from a building or a facility.

Most of us have been in a church building alone. It's usually a dark and scary place when all the lights are out and there is no one but you hearing all the little noises. There is not much love and hope in a dark and empty building. Vision statements are to be lived not hung on a wall to be read. They have to be realized in the hearts of your people and then downloaded to a hurting world. This is the fusion of God's story with our story; it's where God becomes tangible within the hearts of His people to reveal something very wonderful. It's where God's nature reaches out to touch the hurting single mother, caresses the young child torn by divorce, offers hope to the addicted, and life to the suicidal who is giving church one more try. It's where we become God's vision and where His DNA becomes our DNA. It becomes the fulfillment of I John 4:17 where it says that because as He is, so are we in this world.

One of the top items that is brought up when talking about establishing excellence in the church is the need for money. Solomon had a lot of money and it seemed that to provide excellence you would need a lot of money. Granted we may not have the funds that Solomon possessed to elaborately supply our churches, but this should not be our foremost concern. Serving with an excellent spirit has never cost any monetary funds. Some people may say that you have to have money to be excellent, but excellence starts inside the heart of man, not as a result of a cash infusion. You have to begin with the heart and truly desire to serve the people that attend your church. Solomon's heart changed as he gained wisdom, not as he gained wealth.

Proverbs 3:13-18

Happy is the man who finds wisdom, And the man who gains understanding; 14 For her proceeds are better than the profits of silver, And her gain than fine gold. 15 She is more precious than rubies, and all the things you may desire cannot compare with her. 16 Length of days is in her right hand, in her left hand riches and honor. 17 Her ways are ways of pleasantness, and all her paths are peace. 18 She is a tree of life to those who take hold of her, and happy are all who retain her.

Solomon knew that if he were able to obtain wisdom he would have the most important thing. All the other things in life would come as a direct result of receiving wisdom. Riches and honor came as a result of wisdom, not wisdom as a result of riches and honor. There are many wealthy people that don't have a lick of wisdom. We don't need to have riches to show the wisdom of God to our first time visitors, we just need a heart to serve and a heart that desires excellence. Solomon understood that the principal thing was wisdom and even though the Queen of Sheba may not have, she inescapably experienced it. Her experience within the kingdom of Solomon brought about a conversion so to speak. She had heard of all the wonders of Solomon, but now she was a believer. No longer did she need to hear reports about his kingdom, for now she had experienced the kingdom in all it's splendor and was left breathless.

As you pursue excellence to serve your first time visitors, and those that attend your church, get wisdom. By following Solomon's example we too can make believers out of first time visitors by using the same inspiration that Solomon used… the inspiration of excellence.

If we really understood the value of our serving and how it affects salvations of those visiting our churches, would we be more intentional?

CHAPTER TWO

THE FIRST IMPRESSION

"**F**irst impressions are lasting impressions" or "You never get a second chance to make a first impression." I even like the sayings of, "A picture is worth a thousand words" and "Smile and the whole world smiles with you." These sayings are all based around the inspiration of creating something wonderful in a bite size moment. Creating a great first impression can incorporate so many complexities and can make us nervous just thinking about all the things we have to do, be, or look like. There are so many books, articles, presentations, workshops, business consultants, appearance gurus, and seminars that all encompass teachings and motivations for us to create the perfect first impression.

Can you remember a great first impression? What made it so great, inspiring, or left you wanting to know more? Maybe you met someone that just captivated you, or maybe you heard a speech that inspired you to make a difference, or maybe it was a memorable television commercial. One of the most memorable television commercials for me was an ad that ran during the 2000 super bowl. The commercial was an E*TRADE commercial called "Monkey". It showcased two guys in a garage, one older and one younger clapping to a Mexican folk song called "La Cucaracha" as a chimpanzee dressed in an E*TRADE t-shirt danced between them on a five gallon bucket. The spot concluded with the words, "Well, we just wasted two million bucks. What are you doing with your money?" It was so shocking, in that it actually acknowledged something that all of us were already thinking. We were amazed that this company, whatever it was, just spent 2 million dollars for a 30 second spot on 2 guys clapping and a monkey dancing. We were intrigued with this mixed trio of nonsense trying to find out what they were selling, that it never occurred to us that this nonsense didn't have any other purpose except what we were seeing. We had no idea that they were luring us in with the craziness, holding our attention, so they could deliver the message. The ad agency knew that if they could appeal to our natural senses, no matter how irrelevant it was, they would earn the right to deliver their message. We waited in anticipation for the message to come, and eventually it exceeded our expectations. Ever since that super bowl ad ran, E*TRADE has still produced great commercials. The monkeys were hilarious, and the babies captivated us drawing us in to see what was going to be said next. Financial investing is a serious issue, and though monkeys and babies do not invest, nor would they be your first choice of a financial consultant they capture your attention, make you laugh, and actually make you want to know more about E*TRADE. During the super bowl of 2000, it was a great first impression of a company I was unfamiliar with, and I've never forgotten E*TRADE since. The super bowl commercial eventually went on to be one of the top super bowl ads of all time.

Like the ad agency who knew they needed to appeal to the natural first, we too, as we appeal to the natural senses of our first time church visitors will earn the right to deliver our message to them. We have to look at it as, first the natural and then the spiritual. Our message, much more important than financial investing is the message of the Gospel. It's the message of life, hope, restoration, and it's the message of love. Shouldn't we take much more aggressive and intentional planning in our approaches if the Gospel is on the line, rather than financial investing? If we really understood the value of our serving and how it affects salvations of those visiting our churches, we would be more intentional. We have the greatest message that was ever written to deliver; yet sometimes we struggle with earning the right to deliver it. We should do anything within our power to earn the right to deliver the greatest message prepared for mankind.

If you knew that you were about to receive something so wonderful, that was such an awesome power so potent and magnificent that the whole entire world could be changed by it, what would you do? This something would restore marriages, bring comfort to the homeless, food to the hungry, bring joy and healing to the broken hearted, and freedom to so many desperate and hurting people. What if you were given this awesome power and only had one chance to give it to the world. How would you prepare to deliver it?

The church building is the primary tool that most churches use to deliver the greatest story ever told. It's the time where we try to invite the whole community in to receive of the life changing message of the gospel. We spend a lot of money on billboards, radio spots, television commercials, newspaper ads and more to tell people about how great God and our churches are, and how their life can be changed if they just come for a visit. I question how prepared we are in the event they actually showed up. Granted most of our church members that have been attending our church for years will overlook a lot of things, but that's not our target audience. Are we preparing for visitors? Is the process in which we have designed our pre service, service, and post service experiences designed to create a first and lasting impression that captivates and reaches first time visitors, and brings them back for more. A second time visitor presents the greatest opportunity to grow your church, and you can't get a second time visitor without reaching the first time visitor, and you won't reach a first time visitor without a great first impression.

So what is a first impression? Merriam Webster describes an impression as the effect or influence that something or someone has on a person's thoughts or feelings. So a first impression is that first effect or that first influence of a person's thoughts or feelings. It's the first alteration of the senses from an outside influence. It's the first imprint or stamp that you put on someone. It's the moment in time where your mind and emotions receive an imprint, an impression that gives way to a feeling, which then corresponds to a judgment. It's that split second you meet someone for the first time and determine if you like them or not. Think about your spouse, best friend, or the church you now attend. They all did or said something that made you like them and want to engage in more. Some have said that this decision takes 3 seconds, some say just a few minutes. Regardless of whether a first impression happens in seconds or minutes it happens very quickly. The fact is, intentional or not, a first impression is a lasting impression.

How many first impressions do you have in a day? With this thought in mind I was driving down the road and started to take notice. I literally couldn't keep track of all the first impressions I was receiving. You have a first impression every time you see something new. When you see a new sign, when you see a new mailbox, when you see a new person, a new salesperson, a TV show, or when you hear a new song. Have you ever recieved a first impression after reading a few pages from a book? We have hundreds of first impressions every single day. Marketing gurus spend hours upon hours designing a certain billboard advertisement or a flyer for a new ad campaign. They spend the money and the time for the purpose of capturing the right first impression. It's the impression that hooks you in to want to know more, to see more, or to feel more. I have spent years in the advertising field painlessly trying to come up with the right design for a magazine ad. It takes a lot of time to come up with layout, colors, content, font size and style, and the right photos. The advertising world knows that you only have a split second to make a mark on someone's thoughts or feelings. They want to make those seconds count and it's all designed to get your money. Creating the right first impression is not easy, and I think the attitude that people will be attracted to our godliness will override and supercede our lack of excellence sometimes is prevalent. We cannot sacrifice excellence on the altar of sincerity, and be lazy in our approach to presenting the greatest message ever told. If you want to create a great first impression it will take effort, and will take hours to think through how to do it effectively. Your ministry teams will need to buy in to the fact that God is counting on them to deliver His message, and they can't deliver His message without earning the right first.

Have you ever walked into a model home? Model homes are designed to create great first impressions. The realtors know that if they can create a great first impression there's a good chance that you will purchase a home from them. Model homes are designed to hook you in and make you say that this is the home you want to live in. My wife and I had this experience just recently as we walked into a model home and loved it. About a month later we had purchased the model and have made it our own. They had staged the home beautifully with high-end furniture, elegant pictures, and warm accents and of course the home smelled nice. The home was very appealing to our natural senses, and offered us a glimpse of what it would be like to live in the home. A good first impression in regards to buying a home begins with the appearance of the outside of the home. Realtors will tell you that if potential buyers cannot get passed the way the outside looks they will never get a chance to show the inside of the home. You have to have the outside offer an appealing invitation to come in. In the housing market you would call this curb appeal and staging. Our churches are the same way. We must have an appealing invitation from the outside, or we may never have the opportunity to show the community the inside. With the same train of thought we must be individually appealing from the outside, or we may never get the opportunity to show the world what is on the inside of us. We have to generate a great first impression whether it's our marketing, our facility, or our ministry teams. The gospel message is on the line and our churches should not have a disparity in regards to the preparation of the gospel. Remember that this is the greatest message known and given to man. We have to ask the question, "How are we preparing to deliver this life changing message."

If a first impression is the first effect or influence that something or someone has on a person's thoughts or feelings, then what kind of effect or influence do we have on our visitor's thoughts or feelings? Many people visit churches each Sunday but never return. Could it be that we lacked in providing the first impression that would bring them back. What did they think or feel while they were visiting? When we look at our facility or our ministry teams, have we thought about how they will affect the thoughts and feelings of those that walk through our church doors for the first time? God has given us the opportunity to imprint or stamp His impression onto the lives of those in a world that needs Him. Sunday morning or your weekend services offers you the greatest opportunity to make an imprint on the community. It's your time to shine. It's game day so to speak, and we have to be "all in" to provide the greatest first impression possible.

Though it is not fully understood how King Solomon welcomed the Queen of Sheba into his kingdom it is implied that he created a first impression that was beyond what she could have ever imagined. She had probably thought about this welcome at great lengths prior to her arrival and came in with great anticipation. It was going to be her first time to his kingdom and the first time to meet with the King personally. A queen would have had many advisors educating her and coaching her on customs and traditions, along with how she was to present herself and make herself known. She had prepared not only to be impressed but also to impress. She was prepared to meet King Solomon and to provide a first impression of her own. I Kings 10:1-3 tells of the queen's entrance and how she had prepared to meet Solomon.

I Kings 10:1-3 (NKJV)

Now when the queen of Sheba heard of the fame of Solomon con-cerning the name of the Lord, she came to test him with hard ques-tions. 2 She came to Jerusalem with a very great retinue, with camels that bore spices, very much gold, and precious stones; and when she came to Solomon, she spoke with him about all that was in her heart. 3 So Solomon answered all her questions;

The Queen had heard about the fame and wealth and came prepared to test him with hard questions. Just this statement alone tells me that there was great preparation in this visit. She was not coming on a whim or unprepared, but quite the contrary was ready with hard questions that she was hoping he may not be able to answer. She was seeking to know Solomon's limits, where his wisdom ended or maybe even to explore weaknesses. It's funny that when people hear great things about our churches or a particular minister that sometimes they don't believe the stories or what they have heard. They will come to church prepared to find the weaknesses or to prove what they have heard is not the truth. Sometimes these visitors are well prepared to critique the message and every element of your serving teams. They are seeking to find something wrong. It's so exciting when those folks come through the doors and the church is more prepared then they are. It's a great experience when the church can exceed their expecta-tions and actually turn their heart toward God. They may have come in with a heart to test like the Queen of Sheba did, but they leave with a heart that believes.

The Queen didn't only come prepared to test Solomon with her words, she also came prepared to impress with her entourage. She came into the kingdom with a very great retinue or train the bible says. This retinue represented an army of people that accompanied the Queen on her journey and the scripture says that this retinue was very great. This very great army of people was commissioned to serve the Queen and was to bring comfort to her and to provide for her needs. The word retinue also represents strength, wealth, might, force, and efficiency. The view of the queen entering was like a forceful army of strength, wealth and efficiency. This is a very impressive endeavor for the queen to be traveling great distances with such a display by her side. This verse also says that she entered with camels that carried spices, very much gold, and precious stones. These gifts represented her wealth and what she had to offer the King, and undoubtedly would be used in trading practices. This element of the story sheds light on the fact that as we look into our community, we not only see the Queen of Sheba's that want to come into our churches and test us, but we also see some that come in wanting to impress.

We have no idea what is going through the mind of a first time visitor. I try to think about what actually made them come to church that day. I think about the prayers of their families, the divine appointments that God brought into their lives at different times, the way God has spared them from things and positioned them to be reached with His message. Then one day all of this comes together, which may have taken years to culminate into a first time visit. God is now entrusting us, the church, with this person. He is entrusting us with this person who He has been working on for years. He has brought them through a series of life events to finally decide to give God a try and come through our doors. This is a moment of truth for us, as now God has handed this precious soul to us to care for. It's a transition, like the transition for a baby out of the incubator and now into the arms of a loving mother. It's an amazing responsibility to know that God has just delivered to us a child that needs love, care, acceptance, and ultimately a nurturing family. This all takes place the moment they walk through your churches front door. Your greeters, which we call our Welcome Team, need to know that they are the first arms that God is delivering this new child into. Your greeters have such a huge role in what will take place in this person's life at church. What if the new baby was removed from the incubator and delivered to the new mom, but the mom didn't reach out to receive the child and the child was left to fend for itself? What kind of experience would that be for the child? Looking at this from God's perspective in delivering this person now to our care, how do you think God would feel if we dropped the ball as soon as God handed it to us? How do you think God would feel knowing what He went through to get them to try church, and the moment they come in, they are not welcomed and feel alone? We will touch more on this in later chapters, but people don't want to be greeted, they want to be welcomed! Nobody gets connected or builds a relationship around greetings. This is the reason we no longer have greeters at our church and have instituted a Welcome Team instead.

It's interesting to see that as the queen was welcomed into the kingdom and inevitably had a wonderful first impression that she opened up and spoke to Solomon about all that was in her heart. It's the love of God that breaks down the walls and allows people to be themselves. It's the love that we show the people as they walk in the doors that disarms their defenses, and breaks the walls the enemy has built up in their lives. As our ministry teams break down these barriers in our first time visitors you will see an opening of their hearts, and before you know it they will be sharing all that is in it. People need a safe place to be loved and accepted, and people really do want to share with you what is in their heart. It's the loving first impression that lays the foundation and framework that allows people to feel like they can be themselves. It's the first impression that makes people feel they are wanted, and it's the first impression that makes people feel they belong to something special.

One of the best ways to institute a great first impression is with your leadership team, and helping them realize that they are the mission statement of the church. People say that vision leaks, but so does mission, and keeping the mission on the forefront of our hearts will help fulfill the mission. Our mission statement is that we are an oasis of love and hope in a world of darkness and hurt. So I remind myself that "I" am an oasis of love and hope, not the building where we meet. I have to provide love and hope to a hurting world, our building will not. This helps me to have the right countenance and demeanor and places me in the right spirit to minister to those that provide me the opportunity. What is your church's mission statement? Can you be the mission? Can your ministry teams accurately express to your church visitors what your mission statement is, without telling them or having them read it on the wall? This is a challenge for all of us, as we become the church accurately conveying to a hurting world the mission and vision of Jesus seen through the eyes of our local body.

As Jesus engaged people for the first time, He made incredible first impressions on those that he encountered. How do you think the woman caught in adultery felt as she is brought before Jesus, and He disassembles her accusers while writing on the ground? Or what about the woman at the well? Jesus asks her for a drink, which was customarily wrong since she was a Samaritan. He was providing an immediate first impression that she was accepted with him even though he was a Jew and Jews don't have any dealings with Samaritans. Jesus goes on to read her mail and tell her that He is the Christ. He left such an impression on her that she drops her waterpot, runs into the city, gathers the men of the city to come and see if this was really the Christ. With a strong first impression it opens the door for Him now to minister in that city and ends up staying there two days and many of the Samaritans came to be believers. Then there is Zacchaeus, the chief tax collector who was very rich. Zacchaeus, being a short man climbs a sycamore tree to see Jesus as He walked by, not expecting anything but to see Him. Jesus sees Zacchaeus up in the tree and speaks to him to come down from the tree, because He wants to visit with him in his home. Luke 19:6 states that Zacchaeus hurried down the tree and received Jesus joyfully. What a great first impression! A rich sinner receiving Jesus joyfully is a great testimony any time of the day.

Out of all the first impressions that Jesus made the best one was on a man named Saul. Saul was journeying near Damascus, and suddenly a light shone around him from heaven. Then he fell to the ground, and heard a voice saying to him, "Saul, Saul, why are you persecuting Me?" Jesus shines His light and drops an opening line on Saul that brings him to the ground. You can't get much more of a first impression than that. Jesus came on the scene quickly and boldly to bring Saul to his knees. He needed to get Saul's attention and I think it worked just the way it was intended. Saul takes away from this first encounter a new revelation of whom Jesus was. Though it was dramatic with a bright light, audible conversation, trembling, astonishment, and loss of vision, Saul found the Lord. This was a first impression that would have changed anyone's life.

Acts 9:3-9 (NKJV)

As he journeyed he came near Damascus, and suddenly a light shone around him from heaven. Then he fell to the ground, and heard a voice saying to him, "Saul, Saul, why are you persecuting Me?" 5 And he said, "Who are You, Lord?" Then the Lord said, "I am Jesus, whom you are persecuting. It is hard for you to kick against the goads." 6 So he, trembling and astonished, said, "Lord, what do You want me to do?" Then the Lord said to him, "Arise and go into the city, and you will be told what you must do." 7 And the men who journeyed with him stood speechless, hearing a voice but seeing no one. 8 Then Saul arose from the ground, and when his eyes were opened he saw no one. But they led him by the hand and brought him into Damascus. 9 And he was three days without sight, and neither ate nor drank.

We may not be Jesus and can bring people to their knees with our presence, but we can serve in ways that impress upon the heart of the people that they are loved, cared for, accepted in all their mess, and that we want them to be a part of our family. We have to work hard at creating that feeling in our first time visitors that we are glad that they have come to visit us. In fact, research indicates that a new church visitor will make a decision within the first 7-10 minutes whether they will be returning the next week. The first 10 minutes of a church visitors experience actually caters to the person's soul realm, the realm where their 5 senses live. They are gathering that "feeling" to determine their return, whether they want to or not. While this is not very spiritual, it is the reality that we live in. Everyone gathers that feeling, and everyone gathers that first impression. Make yours count!

Your system,
whatever it is,
is perfect for the
result you are
obtaining.

CHAPTER THREE

FROM THE PARKING LOT TO THE ALTAR—SYSTEMS THINKING

Years ago a good friend of mine, Brad Larson, asked me a crazy question. This question changed my life and how I view ministry, and has become one of the cornerstones by which I challenge and train others in ministry. The question was simply, "How do you eat a peanut butter and jelly sandwich?" I looked puzzled, of course, since we were grown adults and assumed that both of us had eaten our share of peanut butter and jelly sandwiches. I humored him, and started off with hand gestures, that you put the knife in the peanut butter... that was as far as I got when he stopped me, and gestured back that I might want to take the lid off the peanut butter jar first. It was like a light bulb went off in my head, a moment of truth for me and quite humbling to realize that when thinking about ministry I was missing a lot of details. The question was in context of projects and getting things done, and to get things done right you will need to see the details. This question opened up to me an element of ministry called "Systems", that I had not seen before and one that would actually produce the greatest results when mastered. I thought ministry was just about visiting people in the hospital, preaching a powerful message, creating new believers, discipling new believers, starting

29

new ministries, encouraging those you came in contact with, and the usual church stuff. What I didn't realize is what takes place to make it all happen. I just liked to eat peanut butter and jelly sandwiches, I never really thought about how I made them, or the multiple steps it really took from the time you wanted the sandwich to the time you actually ate it. Thinking about details can be exhausting, but if the sandwich or ministry is worth it, you will go through the steps to make it.

To illustrate the point, what would the steps look like for you right now if you wanted to make a peanut butter and jelly sandwich? If you really listed out each detailed step separately, you may be amazed at how many there are. Here is my list from where I'm sitting in my office right now writing this chapter.

Go from my office to the kitchen pantry

Open the pantry door

Grab the Smart Balance Rich Roast
    peanut butter off the shelf.

Back up and close the pantry door
    (If you're married this step is extremely crucial)

Take the peanut butter and place the jar
    on the kitchen counter

Now go to the fridge

Open the refrigerator door
    Grab the Welches grape jelly off the shelf

Back up and close the refrigerator door
    (Another crucial step if you're married)

Take the jelly over to the counter where you placed
the peanut butter and put it beside it.

Now go to where the bread is stored

Open the cabinet

Grab the bread off the shelf

Close the cabinet (Crucial Step, if you know what I mean)

Take the bread over to the counter where you placed
the peanut butter and the jelly.

Go to the kitchen drawer that has the knives

Open the knife drawer and pull out a butter knife

Close the drawer (Crucial…)

Take the knife to the counter to where you place the bread,
peanut butter, and the grape jelly

Untie the bread and grab two slices out of the wrapper

Place the bread on the counter
(oh snap! I forgot the paper plate)

Leave the bread on the counter

Walk over to the cabinet where the paper plates are stored.

Open the cabinet door

Grab a paper plate out of the cabinet

Close the cabinet door (Do I need to say it…)

Take the paper plate over to the counter to where you
placed the knife, bread, peanut butter, and the

jelly. (It's really important to keep these items
together and in the same location or
otherwise this listing will never end)

Place the bread that you previously put on the counter
and place them on your paper plate.

Open the peanut butter jar and place the lid on the counter

Open the jelly jar and place the lid on the counter

Take your knife and insert it into the peanut butter jar

Scoop a generous portion of peanut butter onto the knife

Remove the knife with the generous portion
of peanut butter and smear the peanut butter
onto one slice of bread (I combined two steps
here... sue me, its my list)

Then take the knife and insert it into the jar of jelly

Scoop a generous portion of jelly onto the knife.
(Watch out here the jelly is slippery and if
you drop any of this on the floor...

All I can say is 30 more steps!)

Remove the knife with the slippery generous portion of
jelly and smear the jelly onto the second
slice of bread. (Another combo)

Then lay the knife down onto the counter
(your wife will kill you for this one)

Take the peanut butter slice of bread and place it on top
of the jelly slice of bread.

With both hands raised in triumph grab the
   masterpiece sandwich with both hands
   (impossible by the way unless you can
   gravitate the sandwich to your raised hands)

Eat sandwich… QUICKLY

The reason you eat quickly is somewhere between steps 38 and 39 one of your kids will inevitably walk in the kitchen and ask you to make them a peanut butter and jelly sandwich. Of course, after you have made the sandwich, there is always clean up, and the steps involved in that, but I think you get the point. There are a lot of details that we miss when we think about things. Whether it is a peanut butter and jelly sandwich or ministry, it is imperative that we see the details and layout the steps that will produce the results we intend.

A system is a series of steps or a series of components that take place, or work in conjunction for a particular result to occur. In reality, whether we know it or not, our entire life is a system and the result you are getting out of life is a direct result from the system you have in place. Systems produce results, and even your non-system is a system. It may be chaotic, but it is still a system, and your system is perfect for the results you are getting. A chaotic system will produce a chaotic result, an organized system will produce an organized result, poor systems produce poor results, a good system produces a good result, and an excellent system produces an excellent result. If you put in place a 5 star system you will produce a 5 star result, in the same way a 2 star system will produce a 2 star result. Your system, whatever it is, is perfect for the result you are obtaining. If you would like a different result in your life, you would need to change the system you are living in. If you want to change a ministry result, you will need to change the ministry system, not blame the result. The result is simply a bi-product of the system that is in place, and is closely related to the saying, "If you have flies in your restaurant, its because you want them there."

I used to work for Chiquita, the fruit company, and was hired to be one of their fruit inspectors in the Gulf Coast region that primarily inspected honeydew melons and cantaloupes. Large containers of these fresh melons would arrive weekly and then the containers would be transported to the area of the port where our inspection offices were located. Once the containers arrived our team of inspectors would need to inspect the fruit and assign the container a grade, which would determine the value of the fruit, how far it could be shipped, and what the sales price would be. A high grade would allow for the fruit to be shipped great distances, and would sell for premium price, however a low grade would create quick decisions to sell locally, and for a lower price. Obviously, Chiquita wanted the best fruit possible, with the highest grades possible, making the most money possible. For Chiquita to produce the excellent fruit they desired, they knew they would have to create an excellent system. If for some reason the fruit didn't match the quality required, there must be something wrong with the system. They understood that if you fixed the system, then you would have fixed the fruit.

My first associate pastor role put me in a position to be over 5 ministry teams and leaders who were all volunteers doing the best they could with the time they had. I had never been an associate pastor before and I remember getting frustrated early on with one of the leaders for not leading the way that I thought he should be leading. I made a rookie mistake and jumped in to take over the work and figured I could do it better myself. It wasn't long after I had done this that I couldn't sleep one night, so I made my way into a spare bedroom and opened up my bible. I felt like the Lord wanted to share something with me, so I did one of those bible roulette things, and with eyes closed I opened up the bible and pointed my finger onto the page. I know it wasn't very spiritual, but God met me where I was, and my finger landed on Ephesians 4:11-12 which states, "And He Himself gave some to be apostles, some prophets, some evangelists, and some pastors and teachers, for the equipping of the saints for the work of ministry, for the edifying of the body of Christ." I knew immediately what the Lord was saying to me as a new pastor, and I knew what I needed to change in regards to these new leaders that I was overseeing.

Besides stealing this leaders blessing by jumping in and doing the work of the ministry, I was not fulfilling my scriptural duty to equip, and therefore robbing myself of a blessing. Pastors were not only to do the work of the ministry, but to equip the saints to do the work of the ministry. This was a new revelation to me about my role as a pastor and led me down a new path of education to learn how to equip instead of doing. I didn't know how to equip others to do; I just knew how to do. I had gone through years of Bible College, which taught me how to do, but nothing really taught me how to equip others to do. I now had to learn how to get things done through others and give away the ministry.

I was reminded during this time about my role at Chiquita and the process that was involved in creating a great product. I didn't ever look at the fruit and blame the fruit for its condition. It would look rather silly for me to pick up the fruit and blame the fruit for it ripening to soon, or for it to be too yellow, or the appearance to be unacceptably inconsistent. Never did I blame the fruit. On the contrary 100% of the time the problematic issues with the fruit were found in the system. Often times the container coming across the Gulf of Mexico incurred too high of a temperature, causing the fruit to ripen to quickly. Other times the issues were found in the native country with the farmers and growers and their processes, or the miss handling of the fruit. Whatever the problem the fruit had, it was always a result of the process. The system created the result.

When I looked at the ministry and ministry leader, and the lack of leadership that he was exhibiting I was getting frustrated and blaming him for his deficiencies. One day I felt the Lord ask me, "What system do you have in place to produce the leader you want?" It was a challenging question, since I didn't have a system. I hadn't even thought about a system of leadership development. I realized that as I had never blamed the fruit for its lack of quality, I was also not to blame my leaders for their lack of quality. How was I supposed to blame the leader for their lack of great leadership, if I had never created a system to produce great leadership? It didn't take me long to come to the awareness that I was the problem and not this volunteer leader, and confirms the saying that, "A message changes thinking, a system changes behavior."

Salvation begins in the parking lot, is a phrase that I like to say to remind me about our processes and how important the first 7-10 minutes of a first time visitors experience is. If you think about that, you will realize that within the first 10 minutes of their visit the visitors have never heard the preaching, or experienced your worship service, which most churches place the most concentrated effort on. There are a lot of factors in preparing one's soul for salvation, but a great first impression at your church is key, and there is no better place to start than the parking lot.

So what does your church's first 10 minutes look like for the first time visitor? Usually this will begin in the parking lot as they enter your church grounds. It's not a bad idea to place yourself in their shoes if you really want to experience what they are experiencing. Start by driving in your church's parking lot and taking a lot of notes about what you see and feel. After parking your vehicle, take the journey that your visitor would take, looking at the surroundings, the building, signage, landscaping, entryway, again taking a lot of notes on what you see and feel. You will have to remind yourself that your visitors are gathering a "feeling" as they experience your first 10 minutes, whether they know it or not. It will be up to you to create the feeling that you want them to experience through your first impression system. As you continue your journey to place yourself in their shoes, you will enter the church doors. What are the first things that you see? Is it clear where the sanctuary is located, or where the nursery or kids rooms are? Your process will continue as you move through the steps of your visitor by going to the restrooms, coffee bar, information center, hallway, and sanctuary taking notes the whole time. Taking these steps is good for those in leadership to do since familiarity is our enemy. Think back about our example of how we make a peanut butter and jelly sandwich and look for the details. Buried within our minds, we think others see what we see, we think that they don't see the little things because we don't see the little things.

A first time visitor to your church is on high alert; every sensory perception has been charged and ready to see every detail regardless of how small. They will see and feel things due to their sensitivity that you and I would never see or feel. Small pieces of trash in the parking lot, dirty windows at the entrance, carpets not vacuumed, light bulbs burned out, ceiling tiles stained, restrooms not adequately supplied, no one to welcome them at the doors or help them check in their children to the kids church become extreme visual flaws to a first time visitor. As you walk through the first 10 minutes of your church visitors experience what did you see? Did you see wisdom through this process? Was the flow of the journey you have required the first time visitor to take, a journey that will provide a great first impression?

The first 10 minutes is a system, and since a lot of your visitors are making a decision whether or not to return, it may be a very important system to master effectively. Your first 10 minutes represents a dependent system, as each component of the first 10 minutes is dependent on the other. Dependent systems are those systems that require or depend upon other components for them to be successful. If you view the first 10 minutes as independent components than each one will have to carry the load themselves in creating the great first impression that makes the first time visitor want to return. In the church arena, each of our ministry components are always dependent upon the other. A couple with 3 kids visiting for the first time may have a great experience parking on your grounds, but then could have a disastrous experience finding the kids check in stations or kids facilities and choose not to return. Or they could have a frustrating parking experience, but then have a pleasant experience once inside the facility, but still choose not to return due to the parking issues. Each ministry area hands off to the other intentionally to eventually bring first time unbelieving visitors to become fully devoted followers of Christ, serving the Lord with their giftings and passions.

If this first time couple we mentioned earlier with the 3 kids has a bad experience in your parking lot, it will be difficult for your greeters at the door to overcome the parking lot bad impression. With a bad parking experience this couples first impression level is low, and will need to have the other areas pick up the slack to salvage this visit, if they are to return as second time guests. A bad first impression though is very difficult to overcome. This is where the dependencies come into play. Each area depends on the other ministry areas to create great first impressions. You win as a team and you lose as a team and each team member is dependent upon the other to carry their weight.

The Queen of Sheba mentions all the different ministry areas that King Solomon had instituted that formulated into a great first impression. All of these ministry areas came together to create one extraordinary experience for her and her retinue. She lists out the areas from the way his house looked, the food on his table, the way his servants sat, the service of his waiters and the way they were dressed. She even lists out his cupbearers. All of the ministry areas were working together in excellence to lead the Queen on a journey that would bring her to believe all that she had heard. It was a system that was designed to produce a particular result. That day the kingdom of Solomon won as a team. There wasn't one area that was excellent, while the others faltered. All the areas were working in harmony dependent upon each other to create an extraordinary experience, that was beyond the expectation of a skeptical, unbelieving, first time visitor.

I Kings 10:4-5 (NKJV)

And when the queen of Sheba had seen all the wisdom of Solomon, the house that he had built, 5 the food on his table, the seating of his servants, the service of his waiters and their apparel, his cupbearers, and his entryway by which he went up to the house of the Lord, there was no more spirit in her.

As Solomon had all his ministry teams working together for a common purpose, we too need our ministry teams working with the same DNA. We can't have a really awesome parking lot ministry and then falter with a poor Welcome Team or greeters. Each ministry team should have the same heart, same passion, and same DNA to work together as one body functioning for one purpose. As the parking lot ministry fulfills their ministry with excellence, a great first impression is in the making. It is the beginning of your system and starts the process of the results you are intending and praying for. As the visitors flow through the first 10 minutes think about what ministry teams they will encounter. These teams make up your first impressions ministries, which most likely would be consisting of, depending on your church, the parking lot ministry, grounds keeping, greeters, information team, hospitality/coffee bar, kids check-in process, cleaning team, and possibly ushers. Grounds keeping and cleaning teams may not be people they encounter during the first 10 minutes, but their ministry is definitely seen and experienced by the visiting guests to your church.

Great experiences throughout the first 10 minutes lays a foundation that prepares people for worship, and worship prepares people for the Word, and the Word produces salvations and changed lives. Each ministry team that touches your visiting guests, will hand off to one another a precious soul that God desires to touch and change. God is entrusting us, the church, to take their hands and walk them through the journey to salvation and maturity. As we create a great parking lot experience, and then hand off to a great greeting experience, which hands off to a great hospitality experience, which hands off to a great kids check in experience, which hands off to a great ushering experience, which hands off to a great worship experience, which hands off to a great message that produces salvation and a changed life, salvation would have begun in the parking lot. So as it pertains to the first 10 minutes for your first time guests, how do you make a peanut butter and jelly sandwich?

Why is it that we have this innate desire to be served with excellence, yet at the same time we have a tendency to serve others with minimalism?

CHAPTER FOUR

THE CULTURE OF MEDIOCRITY

When you look at Solomon's life you will find that mediocrity was not a trait that neither he, nor his kingdom would be described with. Mediocrity did not have a place in Solomon's heart, and certainly didn't show up in the appearance of his kingdom or how the kingdom was administrated. The Bible says in Philippians that whatever is true, whatever is noble, whatever is right, whatever is pure, whatever is lovely, whatever is admirable—if anything is excellent or praiseworthy—think about such things. Whatever you have learned or received or heard from me, or seen in me—put it into practice. And the God of peace will be with you. Within these two verses there is not much room for mediocrity. There is actually a challenge in these two verses for us not only to think about things that are excellent, but also to put them in practice.

First of all we have to ask the question, "Why do we settle for mediocrity?" I ask this question not from why we accept mediocre service from others, but why we settle for mediocrity in serving others. In light of the American culture there are a few elements that contribute to a mediocre mindset. One of the most prominent elements in daily life is the indifference of how we as people expect to be treated, and how we as people choose to treat others. Why is it that we have this innate desire to be served with excellence, yet at the same time we have a tendency to serve others with minimalism?

Jesus dealt with the minimalist mentality in Matthew chapter 5 when He said, "You have heard that it was said to those of old, "You shall not murder, and whoever murders will be in danger of the judgment." But I say to you that whoever is angry with his brother without a cause shall be in danger of the judgment. And whoever says to his brother, "Raca!" shall be in danger of the council. But whoever says, "You fool!" shall be in danger of hell fire. He also said, "You have heard that it was said to those of old, "You shall not commit adultery." But I say to you that whoever looks at a woman to lust for her has already committed adultery with her in his heart. He also addresses marriage, swearing, going two miles with someone when they only asked for one, turning the other cheek, giving more clothes than you were asked for, and one of the toughest things to do, He told us to love our enemies. Jesus precedes these verses by saying that unless your righteousness exceeds the righteousness of the scribes and Pharisees, you will by no means enter the kingdom of heaven. The Pharisees and the scribes did what was considered the minimum and Jesus is telling the Jews that unless they exceed what the Pharisees and the scribes do they will come up short entering the kingdom of heaven. Jesus closes Matthew 5 with a challenge that eats at the very core of minimalism when He said, "Therefore you shall be perfect, just as your Father in heaven is perfect." The actual word perfect in this verse is translated "telos" and means to want nothing necessary to completeness. This is a challenge presented to us that as we serve people in the community and our local church, we are to serve them in such a way that brings a completeness to them, not just offer them bare minimum services. Jesus didn't just feed 5 people, he fed 5000, and He didn't have just enough left over, but had baskets full left over. Jesus didn't die just for one man, but He died for all of mankind, and He didn't give His spirit to a few disciples but gave it to all believers.

We can see this minimalism illustrated with the unprofitable servant where Jesus says "Which of you, having a slave plowing or tending sheep, will say to him when he has come in from the field, "Come immediately and sit down to eat?" But will he not say to him, "Prepare something for me to eat, and properly clothe yourself and serve me while I eat and drink; and afterward you may eat and drink?" He does not thank the slave because he did the things which were commanded, does he? So you too, when you do all the things which are commanded you, say, "We are unworthy slaves; we have done only that which we ought to have done." The world's motto is simply that you're a good worker if you've just done your job, but Jesus' motto was that we are unprofitable if we just do our job. We have to reach beyond the limits of what is good enough and ordinary, and reach into the realm of more than enough and extraordinary.

In the business world there is a common expression in our culture that the customer is always right. In reality the customer is not always right, but this phrase makes us feel like we have some higher level of power over those that are serving us at checkout counters or service areas. Not too long ago we were having a morning staff meeting at a local McDonalds. I was standing in line and I noticed an older gentlemen giving one of the managers a hard time about a particular breakfast sandwich he had ordered. The manager was apologetic though confused and offered to make it right at no charge of course to the older gentlemen. The problem was that the older gentlemen had ordered something that was not on the menu. He ordered a variation of a breakfast sandwich and of course no one could have read his mind to know what he was asking for. What we had was a customer asking for a specific variation of a sandwich, which was not on the menu, and that he did not specifically ask for, and then proceeded to get upset at the manager for not being able to read his mind. The question that rings in my heart is, what makes us think that we are entitled to be treated with excellence, and yet in return we have the right to treat people with mediocrity or even worse treat people poorly and believe it's ok, acceptable, and even understood as a way of life. The customer was not right in this case, not even close to being right in this case, and yet the balance of excellence was so lopsided, so misguided, and so indifferent. I believe wholeheartedly that businesses should treat their customers with excellence, but I also believe we should match what we expect, and in return, be an example of an excellent customer.

What is an excellent customer? There have been plenty of books, articles, seminars, workshops, manuals, etc… written about customer service, and how to create the perfect experience for those that come in to our stores to buy something or browse, but why isn't there anything written on the customer's service or how we as patrons could in the midst of our shopping sprees provide an amazing experience for the store workers. Maybe we don't feel there is a need to serve the store employees or business owners since we are so used to being served. Why does excellence have to be one sided? Do we not see an opportunity among the employees to serve in such a way that delivers the wow factor to them and possibly draws them into Christ by our example of excellence? It certainly would be different, and may just be the tipping point for someone to want to know why you are different from all the other shoppers that come in being demanding, self centered, and only caring about their own shopping experience.

I have thought about the many times that I have walked into stores and picked up something off the shelf just to put it back on the shelves in a different location, or unfolded shirts off the racks just to put them back on the racks unfolded or messed up in some way, or leaving the shopping cart in the middle of the parking lot so that an employee (which is a real person by the way) has to chase it down, when I could have easily placed the cart in the shopping cart holding section. When searching online for products I often see a Pay Per Click ad at the top of Google, while also seeing the stores website listed just below the advertisement section. Both links regardless of which one I click on will take me to the same place, however the advertisement section, if I click on it will cost the company money, but the website link below the advertisement section doesn't cost anything to the company. I would like to think that I am being an excellent customer by not clicking on the link that will cost the company money and thus reducing the expenses of the company, which in turn will help them keep their costs down for the consumer. In this case the company doesn't see what I have done, but God does, and I know that I have done what I can to treat the company with the best service I can give from a customer's perspective.

I have found there are four main elements that feed into a culture of mediocrity.

1. A life that is too busy, where you don't have time to do it right.

2. A lack of motivation, where you don't see the value in doing it right.

3. The lack of knowledge, where you don't know how to do it right.

4. A life of laziness, where you don't care if it's done right.

When a compromise of excellence is made you can find at the heart of the compromise one of these four elements.

It truly amazes me how many times you can hear the response, "I'm so busy". Why are we all so busy, and could this be playing into our mediocre society? Have we crowded our lives with so much mediocre stuff that we can't live a life of excellence? Have we chosen to do so much good stuff that we no longer have the capacity to accomplish the great? The promise of the personal computer gave us all the grand vision that we would be able to accomplish more things in less time, giving us more time for leisure. You could say that it was going to open up capacity for us to do and think about what is important. What we didn't count on was that as technology increased so did our ability to accomplish more. The window of opportunity became greater and our innate drive to do more, accomplish more, and be more all of a sudden became a reality. The time we saved with technology was never really claimed for leisure, but instead, commandeered to be filled with more stuff to accomplish.

The inefficiencies of a life that is too busy are numerous. We lack the margin we need to do the right things and do the right things well, and when you lack the time to do things well the natural tendency is to cut corners. You cannot obtain excellence by cutting corners, something will have to give, and your excellence is on the top of the list. This cutting of corners leads to a life of minimalism where we begin to ask ourselves, "What is the least I can do and get by?" Or we say, "What is the least amount of effort I can give to obtain the maximum amount of reward?" More practically speaking we ask ourselves what is the least I can do and still get a paycheck, to win, stay married, or function in society. We justify our busyness by believing that all this stuff we are bound to complete is actually healthy so we figure out how to get it all done. We may come home after a long day at work having completed our tasks and made it through the day, but in what manner did we live our life? Due to our busy lifestyles we have adopted everything instant mentality. We want our food fast, our banking fast, our shopping fast, our meetings shorter, our church services shorter, and the list goes on and on. In reality, if all of these things we do equal life, then why are we in such a hurry to get through it?

Where busyness feeds into the concept that we don't have time to be excellent or to do things right, the lack of motivation feeds the concept that we don't see the value in doing it right. Sometimes the value of something is not readily available or easily seen. If we look back at Solomon and the visiting Queen, what made Solomon so determined to provide such a wonderful experience for his visitor? What value did he see in providing the level of service that he required his team to provide? We can ask the same question about our visitor to our church. What value do we see in our parking lot teams, or our welcome teams? It's usually not hard for your pastoral staff or lead teams to realize the value in their serving, but do your volunteers understand, and are they fully engaged in that value. There really is nothing more important than earning the right to present the gospel message to those that have not accepted Jesus as their personal savior. We earn that right through how we serve the people that visit with us. We cannot serve people in mediocrity and then expect them to understand an excellent gospel. Our serving must line up with what we value, and our values should come from what we believe, and our beliefs should be birthed from the gospel message. Believing in an excellent gospel should equate to an excellent value system, bearing excellent fruit as we serve others. It won't be enough for just the pastoral staff or top leadership to understand the value that each ministry team fully represents. A transfer will have to take place for the lay volunteer to see the value and serve with that value in mind for excellence to manifest among the ministry team. Without the true value of the team being fully embraced by each member, motivation will be lowered and mediocrity in serving will rise.

In addition to busyness and the lack of motivation, the lack of knowledge creates the premise that we don't have the knowledge to do things right. This lack of knowledge can stem from many things such as, faulty training systems, a "wing it" mentality, low educational aptitude, hasty lifestyles, or other aspects that leads to an uninformed culture. The issue with this is that we, the church can't afford to be uninformed on loving our communities or reaching out to those that are hurting. Our ministry teams cannot afford to serve our visitor with the lack of knowledge, when it is readily available. Proverbs tells us the wisdom cries out in the streets and is set up high on a hill where everyone can glean from her. Wisdom is available to all who ask according to the book of James and will not be withheld from anyone. Knowledge, wisdom, and understanding are here for the taking, and with so many lives hanging in the balance and our ability to directly impact the course of those lives, we just cannot settle for the lack of knowledge in serving the people. Serving the visitor and our regular attenders with wisdom, understanding and knowledge provides an environment where you earn the right to speak into their life and allows for the gospel message to directly influence their life for maximum impact.

The last element that fosters a culture of mediocrity is laziness, which says that I don't care to do things right. We all have our times of laziness but have you ever noticed how quickly laziness fades away when there is an exciting reward or incentive attached to the task. My dad used to incentivize me as a kid by promising the "Big Orange Drink" after a stretch of labor around the house. Though the work was tough and boring, I always looked forward to the "Big Orange Drink" after I was done. It helped me do the work right so that I could receive the payoff. When the payoff is absent there is an increase in apathy. Many people just work the 8:00-5:00 daily grind and rarely see the big payoff in the end leading to mentality shifts from a self motivating, self producing society to a lethargic, non producing, entitlement society. When people no longer feel something is worth it, productivity will decrease and the chances are that mediocrity will increase. Our ministry teams need to see the payoff of why they serve, and a great way to do this is to include them in the testimonies that your church receives. If you get verbal compliments or a testimony, a letter in the mail, an email or text about your church, the services, or the environment, you should share this uplifting blessing with your ministry teams. If you have a salvation take place in your church or someone achieves other spiritual milestones, than your ministry teams should share in that victory. It will motivate and encourage your team members to remember why they are serving and the results of serving with excellence.

Mediocre service never inspires anyone and rarely will ever produce an impact on anyone's life. It's the truly thought out intentional servant that will change the lives of those around them and create an attractiveness to the gospel as the solution to a life too busy, a life filled with disappointments and unmotivated initiatives, a culture that has lost it's ability to mentor and father the generations that are rising behind us, and a society that seeks its own gain instead of the betterment of those around us. The church has the greatest opportunity to impact positive change in a culture. One of the most tangible ways to create that change is through laying aside a life of mediocrity, picking up a life of excellence, and then instilling this excellence into your church ministry teams, not just meeting expectations, but exceeding them.

When excellence becomes who you are, and not just what you try to do, unimaginable things can take place in your life and in the lives you'll affect.

CHAPTER FIVE

EXCEEDING EXPECTATIONS WITH MINISTRY TEAMS

As we read the story of the Queen of Sheba and King Solomon it becomes pretty clear that Solomon's servants and ministers operated in the utmost of excellence when it came to serving. It's difficult to take someone's breath away when you serve in mediocrity, and for Solomon's servants, their service was something that became who they were, not just what they did. When excellence becomes who you are, and not just what you try to do, unimaginable things can take place in your life and in the lives you'll affect.

Most every church, even the ones just starting out have some form of ministry teams that are commissioned to perform the duties that will support the Sunday morning worship services. There are ministry teams as basic as just the worship team, ushers, and greeters, to very elaborate ministry teams such as production teams, café/coffee bar teams, and very professional guest service teams. Regardless, if your church is small or large, one thing's for sure: you will need ministry teams to help support your worship services. Keep in mind though; supporting the Sunday service is not the only reason why ministry teams exist. Do you know why the ministry teams at your church exist? Do you really know the true purpose of your ministry teams? In most cases we could on the surface answer these questions with relative ease. I was asked one time what does an insurance salesman sell. Of course, without thinking too much about it, I said that he sold insurance. In reality as I was being mentored, this question was not as easy as it seemed. An insurance salesman may on the surface be selling insurance, but no one wants insurance, and if no one wants insurance than how does he sell it. I have yet to find a single person that choose to purchase an insurance policy, and then shows the policy to all their friends because they are so excited about their new policy purchase. The policy documents are usually with very low enthusiasm, filed away in some filing cabinet in the recesses of your home never to be brought out again unless absolutely needed. The policy itself is not exciting, not to be celebrated, nor shared with enthusiasm with friends. Actually it's quite the contrary, thinking about purchasing insurance is something that can depress us, or for some make downright angry. It's become a necessary evil in our country I guess we could say, since we don't want to live with it, but can't for the most part live without it. So back to my original thought about what an insurance salesman actually sells. An insurance salesman really sells peace of mind, not insurance. We want to know that our lives are protected from a calamity or disaster. We want to know that our financial future is secure and that the storms of life wont wash away all that we have invested in during our lifetime. Insurance gives us peace of mind, and that is what an insurance salesman actually sells.

What does a heating and air conditioning salesman sell? It's definitely not the big ole' metal air blowing contraption on the outside of your house or church building. Nobody wants that metal box on the side of their home or building. You probably guessed what a heating and air salesman sells, which is comfort. Our church just went through a purchase of a large ac unit that supplied heating and air to our lobby area. The price tag was staggering for this metal box that was going to sit on top of the church's roof, where no one would see it. For the price of these units you would think that they would be something that you would show off in the main sanctuary, or on the stage, or make an announcement about, or for that matter even do a skit about so that everyone can rejoice with you on this great purchase. In reality the metal box just sits there on top of our roof, with a bunch of other metal boxes blowing air and making noise. It's a good thing we didn't buy just the metal box or we would have had a very unenthusiastic experience. We bought something that would be a blessing to all who come into our lobby and the warmth it provides in the winter, and the cool air it provides in the summer makes it worth it all. We didn't buy a metal air-blowing contraption to sit on our roof; we bought comfort.

This paradigm shift can also be applied to our greeters, ushers, coffee bar, information teams, cleaning teams, children's ministries, grounds keepers, parking lot attendants, and so on. If you asked one of the greeters, "What does the Greeting Team do?" What would they say? What about if you asked the ushers what does the ushering team do, what would they tell you? I think that the sad thing is that the greeters would say that they greet and the ushers would say they usher, but this is where the church has to grow into a greater understanding of the true roles and identity of the ministry teams. The way I see it the information team does not exist to provide information, the greeting team does not exist to greet, the ushers do not exist to usher, the parking lot attendants do not exist to park cars, and the coffee bar folks don't exist to hand out coffee. I'm not trying to make a play on words, or use semantic algorithms to create a way of thinking, but rather prompt a mentality shift that broadens the scope of ministry, and opens up kingdom concepts to place them at the core of each ministry team. It's about seeing the ministry teams differently so that they act differently. We cannot be the same as we have for the last hundred years and expect to reach a new generation with the greatest message ever revealed to mankind. It's about using King Solomon's example of exceeding expectations so that we can turn unbelieving, skeptical first time visitors into returning believers connecting to our Lord and Savior Jesus Christ for greater kingdom impact. The Queen of Sheba didn't only say that it was Solomon's great wisdom that she heard, but she revealed that what changed her life was the visual wisdom that she saw through Solomon's ministry teams that were serving her. This is a transfer of ministry from the institutionalized way of ministry back to the early church way of doing things.

Many years ago the church took on a very different form of government that changed the way ministry was done and has been done ever since. Jesus, when He established the church built it upon the premise that believers were to do the work of the ministry and that all who believes will go into all the world and share the message of the gospel. It is the Great Commission that commands all who believe on the Lord Jesus Christ to go therefore and make disciples of all the nations, baptizing them in the name of the Father and of the Son and of the Holy Spirit, teaching them to observe all things that I have commanded you; and lo, I am with you always, even to the end of the age. Also in the last chapter of the book of Mark, Jesus encourages the disciples and all disciples to go into all the world and preach the gospel to every creature. He who believes and is baptized will be saved; but he who does not believe will be condemned. And these signs will follow those who believe: In My name they will cast out demons; they will speak with new tongues; they will take up serpents; and if they drink anything deadly, it will by no means hurt them; they will lay hands on the sick, and they will recover. These chapters of Matthew 28 and Mark 16 show us how the early church began and how ministry was accomplished before the institutionalized shift took place.

Around the time of 300 AD Constantine ushered in a new way of doing church and the institutionalized church was birthed. The ministry that was entrusted to believers now was transferred into the hands of the clergy. Instead of saints being equipped to do the work of the ministry as outlined in Ephesians 4, now the ministry fell into the hands of those clergy members that had been equipped. It was the stripping away of the power of the church into a powerless church organization. The power of the church has always been the real church, which is the believers. The believers are the real church and the believers were always the ones that were supposed to "do" the work of ministry. It was now the changing of hands that did the work of the ministry and a deep sway of institutionalism began to set in. To this day, 1700 years later, we are still fighting this warped mentality of institutionalized thinking, which has kept the real church captive for so many years. Time warping backwards past the institutionalization of the church through Constantine, past the Great Commission laid out by Jesus, landing in the courts of Solomon I see a victory not only for Solomon, but a victory made possible by his servants. I doubt very seriously that the Queen of Sheba would have left the kingdom of Solomon a believer, in all that she had heard and seen if the servant teams of Solomon had not showed her his wisdom by the way that they ministered. It wasn't just the King that day that affected the Queen of Sheba the visitor, it was the king's ministry teams that completed the victory and forever changed a woman's life. It's not just Jesus our King that affects lives, but it's His ministry teams that complete the victory for our King. As Solomon and his teams worked together to exceed expectations in order to bring about change, so we work together with our King to bring about change in all whom we have contact with. The ministry is not just for the clergy, but for all who believe, and those that serve on the ministry teams in the church are "in" the ministry.

This was a hard lesson for me to learn years ago when I first began pastoring. As I oversaw various ministry teams I was not particularly happy with one of the teams or their leader, and began to step in to help. What I was supposed to do was engage this young leader and help him grow in his leadership and ministry, but rather I seemed to jump in to do the work myself. Ephesians 4 is pretty clear about how we as pastors are to equip the saints to do the work of the ministry and to help the leaders under us become better ministers and servants. As I read Ephesians 4 I realized that I had to do ministry differently, and I needed to change and become an efficient equipper of the saints. Instead of jumping in and taking over doing the work of the ministry, I now was forced to figure out how to do the work of the ministry through others. Like most other pastors, our education focused on how to do the work of the ministry instead of how to equip others to do the work of the ministry. I had to change, and for any church to realize its full potential, it also will need to change and embrace the concept of equipping instead of the pastors doing all the work.

I guess you could say this comes down to vision. All churches will have a vision statement for their church, but do the ministry teams individually have a vision statement for their ministry? I ran across a vision statement from Starbucks that read, "To inspire and nurture the human spirit - one person, one cup, and one neighborhood at a time." I liked the statement simply because they understood that they weren't in the business of selling coffee. They would use coffee as a means to nurture the human spirit and to affect individuals and neighborhoods. Where we would have answered a simple question about what does Starbucks do, with a quick, "They sell coffee" Starbucks corporate would have a totally different perspective on their business model and ultimately how the company operates. This statement also allows for Starbucks to determine if they have been successful or not. If success were just about selling coffee they would have had a very different vision statement. To Starbucks its about affecting lives in a way they feel is positive, and coffee just happens to be the means to get them to the end.

Starbucks also has individual vision statements for each segment of their business:

Our Coffee

It has always been, and will always be, about quality. We're passionate about ethically sourcing the finest coffee beans, roasting them with great care, and improving the lives of people who grow them. We care deeply about all of this; our work is never done.

Our Partners

We're called partners, because it's not just a job, it's our passion. Together, we embrace diversity to create a place where each of us can be ourselves. We always treat each other with respect and dignity. And we hold each other to that standard.

Our Customers

When we are fully engaged, we connect with, laugh with, and uplift the lives of our customers— even if just for a few moments. Sure, it starts with the promise of a perfectly made beverage, but our work goes far beyond that. It's really about human connection.

Our Stores

When our customers feel this sense of belonging, our stores become a haven, a break from the worries outside, a place where you can meet with friends. It's about enjoyment at the speed of life—sometimes slow and savored, sometimes faster. Always full of humanity.

Our Neighborhood

Every store is part of a community, and we take our responsibility to be good neighbors seriously. We want to be invited in wherever we do business. We can be a force for positive action—bringing together our partners, customers, and the community to contribute every day. Now we see that our responsibility—and our potential for good—is even larger. The world is looking to Starbucks to set the new standard, yet again. We will lead.

Our Shareholders

We know that as we deliver in each of these areas, we enjoy the kind of success that rewards our shareholders. We are fully accountable to get each of these elements right so that Starbucks—and everyone it touches—can endure and thrive.

If Starbucks fulfills the vision of each of their segments they will automatically fulfill the overall vision of the company. This is the same for Church. If each ministry team fulfills their vision, which is based on the overall vision, then the church's vision will automatically be fulfilled.

Starbucks didn't try to meet expectations of what coffee was. If that were the case, they would have charged .99 cents for a cup and called it good. But if your going to charge $4 for a cup of coffee you better show me something I haven't seen before. And they did with the Venti Iced Skinny Hazelnut Macchiato, Sugar-Free Syrup, Extra Shot, Light Ice, No Whip Coffee, and then there is the Quad Grande, Non Fat, Extra Hot Caramel Macchiato Upside Down (don't know what upside down is), and last but not least is the Iced, Half Caff, Ristretto, Venti, 4-Pump, Sugar Free, Cinnamon, Dolce Soy Skinny Latte.

Though Starbucks is not perfect, I do believe they have been a catalyst in changing the way people think about coffee. They raised the bar and unveiled a different kind of coffee house, and certainly exceeded expectations about how coffee should be served.

I believe that as many cutting edge moments in our history had a tremendous impact on society, it's time for the church to raise it's standard, take their moment in time, and take a catalytic step to impact the society we live in. Churches have to change the way they view their ministry teams, and allow their teams to become a revolution for superior influence. A revolutionary and fundamental change in the way a ministry team functions will give rise to a realization that salvation for those walking into our churches begins with the ministry teams, and changing the mentality of how we serve with those teams, will result in greater impact on our world.

Let's take a look at the Greeting Team and the Usher Team as they are usually a churches largest ministry teams, and a few ways to look at them differently. You may have your own ideas, but these can help jumpstart your brainstorming juices. As we follow King Solomon's example to exceed expectations within your ministry teams, ask yourself what the people expect from this ministry team and then exceed their expectations. You will be amazed at the results.

Greeters:

Greeting is one of the most common ministry teams found in churches. It is very rare to visit a church that does not have some form of greeting team or at least a few greeters at the door to greet people as they come in. Since it is the most common of the ministry teams it is also one of the most overlooked ministry teams in light of its importance. I will spend a little more time on the greeters for this very purpose. Remember the question about what does an insurance salesman sell? It's time to ask why does a greeting team exist, and what really is their main function. The most common answer is that a greeting team greets, but I would like to offer a challenge to that prevailing mindset. If you really think about this, you will discover that people would rather be welcomed versus just being greeted. Being greeted and being welcomed are two very different things. So the way I see it, a greeting team exists to create a welcoming environment and you can't do that just by greeting. Take for example someone coming to visit you in your home and as they walk in your front door you greet them. Then you let them fend for themselves. They have no idea what to do next, where the restrooms are, or where they should be seated. This creates a very awkward situation even though you enthusiastically greeted them at the door. The same goes for the church as so many people walk through the front doors of our churches and we greet them thinking that we have done our duty, yet still awkwardness prevails in our visitors and too much awkwardness will solidify the decision to not return.

My wife and I had a first visit to a church of about 150 members, and as we walked through the front doors no one greeted or welcomed us. It was a large foyer with many people around though no one seemed to reach out. We were the visitor and had no idea the layout of the building or where the sanctuary entrance was. I leaned over to my wife and whispered in her ear, "Just keep walking, we'll find it." It was very awkward and left a bad impression on us within seconds of us coming through the front doors.

In studying greeting versus welcoming in our own church setting we have found that people love to be welcomed and greeting no longer satisfies. Though we still say hello to people outside our front doors we have incorporated a welcoming process that strives to exceed the expectations of those God gives us. We have actually changed the name of our team from the greeting team to "The Welcome Team" and have trained our volunteers on the difference between greeting and welcoming. It has been an amazing transformation for our church and for those that visit with us. I think for all of us visiting a new church or for the lost to come for a visit, one of the greatest things that is needed is to feel welcomed. We don't really care about the greeting, but the feeling of being welcomed has an amazing result on our hearts. The feeling of being welcomed somewhere creates a sense of belonging, and that one "fits in" so to speak. It's about an acceptance not a formality. When you welcome me into your home, it makes me feel that you want me there and that I am accepted by your family. Greeting just can't do this for anyone, and comes nowhere close to producing the same result. It is imperative, if we desire to reach the lost, or our visitor, that the church has to change from greeting people to a more effective modification in making people feel welcomed.

As mentioned in an earlier chapter we have no idea what God has been doing in the life of the visitor. God could have been working on them for years, orchestrated divine appointments, inspired family to pray, and coordinated certain events in their life that has brought them to a place to try church one last time, or to brave a visit for the first time. As they come to our church doors God is handing them carefully off to us as a newborn is being handed off to their mother for the very first time. The mother doesn't just greet the newborn, but creates a welcoming environment that makes the newborn feel accepted, wanted, and loved. Your greeting team or welcome team is the first hands usually that accept the "visitor handoff" from God. With this in mind, how important is your greeting team now? I hope that somehow you are inspired to never just greet people, but on the contrary, provide a welcoming experience where your visitor will feel an incredible sense of belonging, and an unconditional acceptance into the family of Christ.

Ushers:

When you think about ushers at the church what do you think about? What are the first few things that come to mind? If you're like me you probably saw a group of men that collect the offering and occasionally help someone find a seat, but in reality are not that welcoming. In following suit with our insurance salesman question, why do ushers in our churches exist? I may have a different way of looking at things but I don't believe that the ushers exist to usher. I would challenge that the ushers are actually "hosts" by definition and exist to create and maintain a friendly, inviting, orderly, and caring atmosphere before, during, and after each service that provides an environment for spiritual growth and for salvations to take place. The "Host Team" is a better name instead of the usher team. Hosting and ushering are very different as ushering performs a formal duty and hosting engages people to extend the welcoming environment created by your greeting or welcome team. So many times if you have managed to create a fantastic welcoming experience it usually doesn't continue once the visitor actually enters the sanctuary. We have seen, and you have too I'm sure, many visitors just sitting by themselves never talking to anyone once they enter the sanctuary. This is another shift in the mentality of ministry teams. Usher ministry usually has not been known to be the team that creates a warm, friendly, or welcoming environment engaging the people. They are usually the ones that maintain order and make sure all the rules are not broke during service. I realize that order needs to be maintained and a safe environment is necessary during our services, but if that is why ushers exist than this is falling way short of their potential as a ministry team.

Let me propose a thought provoking question. What if ushers actually treated the people entering the sanctuary as if the people just entered their personal home? Each usher responsible for a particular designated section of people to act as a "host" to them, engaging them, introducing themselves by name (sort of like a waitress does), and informing the people that they will be serving their section today, and if they need anything to let them know. This would certainly exceed my expectations as I have never experienced that level of care from any church usher. Ushers or "The Host Team" members have such a great and awesome opportunity to provide exceptional service and care, and to extend the welcoming environment that the visitor would be blown away by. Creating a welcoming and accepting environment should be the goal of each and every ministry team. We shouldn't just leave it up to the greeters to make people feel welcomed, every ministry team can exceed expectations and help the visitor and church members feel cared for, loved, and accepted into the family.

Many churches also have information teams which I would say should not just provide information. What does information produce? Most of the time information that information teams provide are opportunities to connect with people. Whether it is information about small groups, activities, special services, or events, all of these present an opportunity to build relationships with others. I would challenge that your information team does not exist to provide information, but exists to connect people with relational opportunities to foster greater spiritual growth and dynamic lifelong friendships.

Parking lot team:

Then there is the parking lot team that helps park cars. In reality are they just parking cars? There was a man who worked on the parking lot team of a large church in Tulsa that said something that was very fascinating and has stuck with me for years. He said, "I don't park cars, I park people." Wow, what an amazing insight into his ministry and really goes along with our insurance salesmen question. This man saw beyond what everyone else saw and made a shift in how he served. Where others saw a non exciting job of parking dirty metal vehicles, he saw the lives that were in those vehicles. It's not so exciting if all you are doing is parking cars, since Jesus didn't die for cars, but when you add the personal element to parking people, ministry is suddenly birthed, and the parking lot ministry takes on a whole different meaning.

There are so many other ministries in our churches to look at differently. We could look at the coffee bar where most just feel they are serving coffee to people, but what they don't see is the environment that they are creating that lets people relax and let their guard down. When our guards are down we let people in and allows for the Lord to move more freely in our lives. There are nursery ministries, children's ministries, media teams, and so much more. Each of the ministry teams represented in our churches have so much potential to change lives. I am always troubled when I hear someone say that they are "just" a greeter or "just" an usher at church. I just want to sit down with them and tell them how valuable they really are to the salvations that take place on Sunday morning. No one is just a greeter or just an usher, they have the greatest opportunity to lay a foundation for salvation then anyone, and I wish they all knew how important their ministry really was. King Solomon's ministry teams changed the life of a very important visitor, and as we use his example, we can change the lives of the very important visitors that God brings to our church's doorsteps as well.

*We cannot pray for
10 gallons of water
and only have a
5 gallon bucket.*

CHAPTER SIX

5 GALLON BUCKET WITH 10 GALLONS OF WATER

Now that you have set, or at least thought about the vision for your ministry teams exceeding expectations, its time to assess whether or not you are ready to execute your vision. It will be difficult to have this great vision for something and then not have the resources, capacity, or margin to fulfill it.

We have all read and heard about companies, CEO's, and entrepreneurs that have had great vision, yet have failed miserably trying to complete the execution of the vision. A quick search on Google of failed startups will reveal a very telling tale of millions of dollars lost, years wasted, and visions unrealized. The real tragedy is that all of it could have been avoided with the right knowledge, understanding, and a certain degree of wisdom. King Solomon, who exemplified all of these qualities, is an example to us by revealing that true success comes when we take care of the visitor. I realize that much can be done with the wealth of Solomon and some may even say that, "If I had great wealth like Solomon, I could be successful too". Going back to that little Google search reveals that the lack of wealth had nothing to do with the failures of many of these companies. Take for example Solar-panel maker Solyndra, who may be one of the highest profile startup failures of all time. The company filed for bankruptcy just after receiving $535 million in loan guarantees. Solyndra had government support, great wealth, a team of executives, and yet still failed to execute their vision. Hiten Shah, Co-Founder at KISSmetrics said that he and his co-founder spent $1,000,000 on a web hosting company that never launched. Hiten shared that their perfectionism drove them to build the best thing they could, without even understanding what their customers cared about. Now, they have learned to spend smart, optimize for learning, and focus on customer delight. Preparation is a key component to business and life success, and even Abraham Lincoln said, "Give me six hours to chop down a tree and I will spend the first four sharpening the axe."

As businesses try to find success by understanding their customers, we the church will have a greater chance of success as well, as we seek to understand the visitor who walks through our front doors for the very first time. The real challenge is for the church to be ready to receive the vision that they are praying for. In proverbs the bible says that the horse is prepared for battle but the victory comes from the Lord. There is a preparation that must take place for us to receive our victory. So many times it seems that we are praying for the vision God has given us, yet we fail to prepare for that vision to become a reality. The victory is clearly from the Lord yet it is interesting that the Lord is still requiring the horse to be prepared. It may seem like a waste of time to prepare for victory in advance that is already provided, but yet there is a kingdom principle in this verse that reveals that we are working with the Lord, not just waiting on the Lord. God is revealing that there is an amazing partnership that we have with Him as he provides the vision or victory for us, and we prepare our facilities, people, and ministry to receive it.

Luke 14:28-31 says, for which of you, intending to build a tower, does not sit down first and count the cost, whether he has enough to finish it, lest, after he has laid the foundation, and is not able to finish, all who see it begin to mock him, saying, "This man began to build and was not able to finish"? Or what king, going to make war against another king, does not sit down first and consider whether he is able with ten thousand to meet him who comes against him with twenty thousand? This verse in context is talking about each of us counting the cost of following Christ, but also provides us with an illustrative example of preparation.

Vision in and of itself can be challenging, but the challenge has never been to have a vision, but to have the right vision. What I have found is that most churches organize their ministry teams for the amount of congregants they currently have in attendance. This represents single vision that seeks to meet the current demands of the church. Its what you see now, which in reality puts you behind the demands playing "catch-up". This leads to a whole slew of problems that we equate to the common phrase "growing pains". Though some of these growing pains cannot be avoided, many of the most critical areas of your church can be prepared in advance to accommodate this growth without experiencing the pain. Instead of positioning yourself and your ministry teams to meet the current demand of your church, why not position your teams to meet the future demand. As your demand grows, instead of scurrying around with volunteer recruitment campaigns in order to fill desperate holes in your ministry teams, it would have been better to have planned in advance for this growth and therefore simply waiting on it.

It is always better to stretch yourself, than to have an outside influence do it for you. When you stretch yourself you can control the pain level and keep it manageable. I would much rather stretch myself then have someone else stretch me. You never want to be behind the eight ball trying to implement changes for a new demand, but instead you want to be ready to receive the demand with open arms. Businesses spend countless hours and millions of dollars trying to fill the cracks where their customers are falling through. We the church have so much more at stake, as we are being entrusted with precious lives that God has created. We use the phrase that people in our church are "falling through the cracks" so nonchalantly that we have lost the conviction that these are lives that we are losing. Jesus Christ went to the cross and experienced terrible pain and suffering for these people and yet we struggle to fill the cracks that lead them back to the world of darkness and hurt.

In assessing your ministry teams for success you will need to look at the future. You will need to get beyond where you are currently, and ask the question of where you want to go. If you or your church doesn't have a vision beyond where you are currently positioned then you need a new vision. God always provides a vision beyond our current status and one that we will need to rely on Him to help fulfill. If you are not sure what your future vision is, let me challenge you to have "double vision". Since attendance is the easy metric, instead of building your ministry teams to handle your current attendance why not build your ministry teams with the capacity, systems, and structure to handle double your current attendance. This provides you with what is called margin.

"Margin" is defined by Merriam Webster as the "spare amount" or measure or degree allowed or given for contingencies or special situations. The extra amount of something that can be used if it is needed. Typically one of the side effects of the lack of margin is stress. Stress levels tend to rise when there is a push at the boundaries and there is no margin to stop the push from going over the edge.

My wife and I took a trip to the Grand Canyon one year for a little get away. We both had never been to the Grand Canyon before and were very excited about going and planned to stay a couple of days there. One of the first things you will notice as you are driving up to the lookouts, is that in some areas there is very little shoulder on the roads and the views are quite breath taking. This doesn't make for such a good combination for the driver of the vehicle as they need to keep their eyes peeled on the road, otherwise they could easily become part of the scenery. The road's shoulder represents margin for the road. It's the extra part of the road that you may need at certain times when you cross the road's boundaries. Even though the road is designed for our vehicles we all know how much the shoulder represents a safety to all of us. Without that shoulder for the road there is very little roam for error, and this is the main factor in the increase of stress levels. The wider the road and shoulder, the less stress we will feel in crossing over into a danger zone.

My wife is a lot less conservative in her adventures than I am. I tend to be the cautious one, which apparently gives her the freedom to venture out to the edges. At one point in our trip we decided that we would walk down the canyon a bit to see if we could get a better angle on some of the incredible views of the landscape. The time of year was cold, and there was still ice and snow on the ground and walking paths, so we bought some ice cleats to put on our shoes so that we wouldn't slip down the narrow paths and fall off the cliffs. We reach this one point where there was a small narrow rock that jutted out to an overhang, which of course is covered in slippery snow, and of course my wife wants to wander out onto. While she is out on this small rock, with no guard rails, or protection whatsoever, she proceeds to stand on one foot while tying her shoe on the other foot. I literally could have passed out at that moment. There was absolutely no margin for error and she could have easily slipped off the cliff. I had read in the gift shop that there had been 600 deaths at the Grand Canyon simply because people had gotten to close to the edge and fell off. I am sure that most thought they were ok, until they started to fall. In the same way many times we think our ministries are ok until we start to fall as well. We have to take a serious look at margin and realize that margin is a friend and not a restrictive enemy.

In looking at ministry teams, if we build our teams to serve the current attendance we won't have margin in the event God answers our prayers and the attendance increases. This leads to a number of negative factors that you will see when evaluating your ministry teams and their leaders. One of those negative factors that you will see with a lack of margin will be more mistakes with your team. It's just not going to be possible for your team or leaders to be mistake free when you have no room for error. We have seen this on more than one occasion with our Welcome Team. We have a certain amount of volunteers serving in a particular capacity on a Sunday morning that specifically caters to our first time visitors. On occasion the amount of first time visitors will exceed our capacity to serve them effectively, creating holes and mistakes in our serving. We say so often that our desire is to reach our city, yet when God begins to answer that prayer and brings us first time guests, we have not really prepared for them. Here is a thought to ponder…. What if this Sunday 5% of your cities population decided to come to your church, or 1% in larger cities? I would assume you are praying to reach at least that. Would you be ready for them, and could you serve them properly.

Another negative factor that will surface as a result of not having enough margin with your ministry teams will be frustration. The inability to cover all the bases for your team when you have a limited amount of team members will create a very frustrating experience for your volunteer teams and their leaders. Everyone wants to serve well and feel that their serving is important for a greater purpose. Because of mistakes and not being able to serve effectively, frustration levels will certainly rise, which eventually will cause you to lose valuable volunteers. It's amazing sometimes that the only real culprit to losing volunteers in ministry could possibly be traced back to margin levels. In addition to higher stress levels, frustration, and increased mistakes you will also find a slew of inefficiencies within your team. Team members may need to cover double duty or extra positions due to a thin volunteer team base and therefore cannot truly focus on their main responsibilities. This is where stuff begins to fall through the cracks as we mentioned earlier, lowering our ability to serve the people and visitor with the care that God has intended for them to have.

Four negative factors you will have when you don't have margin:

- If you don't have margin you will have STRESS.
- If you don't have margin you will have MISTAKES.
- If you don't have margin you will have FRUSTRATION.
- If you don't have margin you will have INEFFICIENCY.

We can see this play out in our daily lives as well. Take for example the feeling that comes over you when your low fuel light comes on, your on the interstate and just passed a gas station a couple of miles back. It's really not a good feeling to know that you are almost out of gas and you have no idea how long before you reach the next gas station. I am sure that at least one of those negative factors is going to rise very quickly due to the lack of margin in the gas tank. What about the feeling when you had to cram for a test or were late for an important meeting? Due to the lack of margin with your time you are now scrambling trying to beat the clock or burn the midnight oil to catch up. Lastly and one of the most frustrating and stressful daily life examples is the lack of margin in our finances. I really don't need to elaborate here, since we all know the negative factors that present themselves when we are low on income and high on expenses.

Margin is a very important factor in life, and it's an important factor with our ministry teams. Your teams need margin, and as you give them the margin they need they will be ready to handle the vision and answered prayers of more visitors to your church. I like the sayings, "Dig your well before you get thirsty", and "It's best to know the emergency plan before the plane is going down", as they so eloquently describe the disaster if not heeded.

The challenge for most churches has always been that they are praying for 10 gallons of water but only have a 5 gallon bucket. It's easy to have a 10 gallon vision for your church, but not so easy to create the capacity, systems, and structure to handle a 10 gallon vision. This is why so many are still praying for the 10 gallons, but have never seen this vision realized in their churches. The vision is not the problem and will never be the problem, since hopefully your vision comes from the Lord guiding you to believe a certain way and for certain things. The difficulty comes in when we don't know how to build the bucket that will hold the water we are believing for. This is a sad reality that we all must overcome and learn from the story of King Solomon and the Queen of Sheba. Solomon had created a system of servanthood that was able to not only serve the normal visitors and residents of the kingdom, but also able to handle the massive influx of the Queen's entourage. You could say that King Solomon was ready, had capacity, developed healthy systems, and formulated structure in advance for whatever came his way.

I believe that healthy things grow and is a representation of the natural progression of life. When something in this life is healthy it will automatically grow. You don't have to force it, manipulate it, and struggle with it to grow. Healthy things just grow naturally. In the same way healthy churches grow and those that have healthy capacity, systems, and structure will allow for stretching and growing with little affect from "growing pains". After all, you are praying for growth. In our example you are praying for 10 gallons of water and now you just need to create the capacity to handle the 10 gallons God is going to send you.

This is so often overlooked with our ministry teams yet is so easily seen in the capacity of our sanctuaries. In America we know that as our sanctuaries begin to fill to the 80% level we have to expand and increase our capacity, otherwise we will no longer grow. We like our space in America and don't like to be crowded. Why is this so simple to understand when it comes to our sanctuary capacity, but yet so misunderstood when it comes to our ministry teams and their ability to effectively care for the visitor, or for your regular attenders?

Your ministry teams need to have capacity, healthy systems, and a healthy structure in place that goes beyond just serving who you have currently attending. This will help in reducing the stress of those entrusted to us falling through the cracks, losing valuable ministry opportunities to nurture, disciple, and mentor. We should be asking ourselves as ministry leaders not what our teams should look like to meet the current need, but what should our ministry team look like to meet twice the current attendance. This will position you with double vision and allow you to build capacity, systems, and structures that will be in place in advance of the growth. Preparing for the growth is much easier than trying to catch up with it.

There is a short activity that I do with our ministry teams to determine an element of their preparedness. It's actually two activities where one reveals a percentage of how prepared we are for our attendees currently, and then the second one determines a percentage of how prepared we are for the future growth and vision of the church that we are all praying for. This activity is based solely on the amount of volunteers and not on other preparedness factors such as volunteer training, leadership development, spiritual maturity, etc. We have found these two activities to be very helpful and eye opening when it comes to determining our volunteer team member requirements. Below you will find the activity and a description on how to accomplish it, in the event you choose to do the activity with your ministry teams.

ACTIVITY 1:

How Ready Is Your Ministry Team With Volunteers?

"Currently"

Create a Box Chart For Your "Current" Status

Step 1: For each ministry team take a sheet of paper and pen and draw a box at the top of your paper and put the ministry leaders name in it.

Step 2: Then for each volunteer team member that you need to meet the current demand, place a box on the chart, below the box that has the team leaders name in it.

For example if you have decided that you need 4 volunteers in this particular ministry team to handle the "current" attendance of your church, in addition to the team leader then draw 4 boxes under the leaders box (as seen in the example). This will give you a total of 5 volunteer positions available to fill.

Step 3: For each team member you currently have on your team, place their name in one of the boxes that is below the team leaders box.

In our example below we only have 2 volunteers on the team besides the leader, (Jill and Mark), but we need a total of 4 volunteers, so the other 2 boxes are left blank with question marks because we have yet to recruit volunteers for those two positions.

Step 4: Last step is to simply divide mathematically the number of "named" boxes by the total amount of boxes to determine your "Readiness" percentage.

SAMPLE – Information Team (to meet current need)

3 named boxes (Joe, Jill & Mark) divided by 5 total boxes = 60% Ready

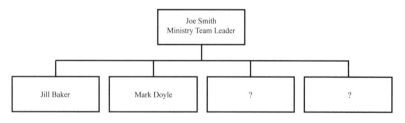

In this first example you can see that as far as volunteers go this team is only 60% ready to handle the current attendance load. This means that they are more than likely on a consistent basis trying to find volunteers at the last minute to help out and/or overworking the current volunteer team, or just not able to serve the attenders and visitors the way that God has intended for them to serve them.

In the second activity below, you will look at the future vision that your church is praying for, and what those demands will look like for your volunteer ministry teams. You will set up a similar box chart (or use the current one and add to it) to visually show how many volunteers your ministry team will need to handle the future demands as God answers your prayers and increases your ability to reach more people.

ACTIVITY 2:

How Ready Is Your Ministry Team With Volunteers?

"Future"

Create a Box Chart For Your "Future" Status

Tip: Use the chart that you created for the "current status" activity and just add to it.

Step 1: For each ministry team take a sheet of paper and pen and draw a box at the top of your paper and put the ministry leaders name in it.

Step 2: Then for each volunteer team member that you need, place a box on the chart, below the box that has the team leaders name in it.

For example if you have decided that you need 7 volunteers in this particular ministry team to handle the "future" attendance of your church, in addition to the team leader then draw 7 boxes under the leaders box (as seen in the example). This will give you a total of 8 volunteer positions available to fill.

Step 3: For each team member you currently have on your team, place their name in one of the boxes that is below the team leaders box.

In our example below we only have 2 volunteers on the team besides the leader, (Jill and Mark), but we need a total of 8 volunteers, so the other 5 boxes are left blank with question marks because we have yet to recruit volunteers for those positions.

Step 4: Last step is to simply divide mathematically the number of "named" boxes by the total amount of boxes to determine your "Readiness" percentage.

SAMPLE – Information Team (based on future vision)

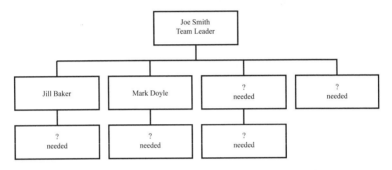

3 named boxes divided by 8 total boxes = 37.5% Ready

In this second example you can see that as far as volunteers go, this team is only 37.5% ready to handle the future attendance load. This simply means that they have a 37.5% bucket while praying for 100%. If all of a sudden the vision is realized one Sunday morning or even over a course of a month, this ministry team will only be 37.5% ready and effective at serving the people and the visitors. Since most of these new people that flooded in would have been visitors, and the ministry team is serving with only a 37.5% readiness, it's doubtful that the visitor will actually feel cared for, resulting in a bad first impression, bad experience, and most likely not return for a second visit. For this ministry team to be able to handle what they are praying for they will need to increase their volunteer base for this ministry team by 62.5%. These numbers are also helpful for the senior pastor or pastoral leadership since they will be able to quantify the preparedness (at least from a volunteer numerical basis) by simply asking the ministry team leaders how ready they are, and the team leaders could respond with a numerical percentage.

The goal here is to be ready for the growth that God is bringing the church. We cannot pray for 10 gallons of water and only have a 5 gallon bucket. If we are praying for 10 gallons of water then we need to prepare now for the 10 gallons and build our ministry teams to support the 10 gallons as well. The reduction in stress, mistakes, frustration, and inefficiencies will go a long way with your ministry teams and the team leadership. This preparation will also posture you for the growth instead of having growing pains playing catch up with the growth. If you wait for the future to prepare for the future it will be too late, so start now, pray for a 10 gallon vision and build a 10 gallon bucket to receive it.

*Is it possible that we
the church have traded
the burden of Jesus,
which is light and easy,
for the burden of man
which is heavy
and difficult.*

CHAPTER SEVEN

BUILDING YOUR MINISTRY TEAM

If you completed the activities from the last chapter you probably realize you have plenty of opportunities for your church attenders to get involved in ministry. The difficult part is getting your attenders to see what you see and inspire them to plug in. There is an innate yearning in each one of us to understand life and why we were created. Our God has made us such intricate beings with an amazing array of personality qualities, emotions, desires, dreams and temperaments. The goal of creation wasn't just to produce a species of mankind that journeys through life trying to find why they were created and what purpose their life may hold. It's much more complex than that, which dives headlong into purpose, intentionality, and strategic design.

So many people struggle with their identity not realizing who they were designed to be, and the purpose their life was created for. They move through the rhythms of life working a career they may not like, and waiting for some relief on the weekends. There was a popular song in the 80's by the pop band Loverboy called "Working For The Weekend" and exemplified a life that was filled with overwork, wanting, pursuit of happiness, second chances, and hoping it will all work out. There is a sense of hopelessness in that song that seems to strike a chord among the populace of our country. We stare curiously in the mirror vexing to find some meaning to this life and our life. Deep within we know there is a greater purpose, and that there is something more than what we are seeing around us, but for most are unable to reconcile the internal sense of purpose with the external reality of the daily grind.

In the book of Jeremiah we see an indication that God has thought about our lives in advance prior to our birth and has intentionally set us up for a unique purpose to complete. Jeremiah 1:5 says, "Before I formed you in the womb I knew you; Before you were born I sanctified you; I ordained you a prophet to the nations." Also, Jeremiah 29:11 says, "For I know the thoughts that I think toward you, says the Lord, thoughts of peace and not of evil, to give you a future and a hope."

It's nice to know that in the midst of our chaos that God has a plan and a purpose designed for each one of us to fulfill, and He has good thoughts toward us to help us complete it. We don't have to go through life with blinders on our eyes not able to see and fulfill the true purpose for our lives. We have a God, Creator, Master Designer, Strategic Thinker, Economist, Creative Planner, and Comforter to help us complete the purpose He has laid out for us. Its when each of us turn in our own plans for His plans, our own desires for His desires, our own will for His will and our own dreams for His dreams, when the real purpose of our lives begins to unfold. Our surrender to the Lordship of Jesus initiates a transfer of ownership of our lives and beckons a new order of living filled with a renewed sense of purpose, hope, and fulfillment. It's at this moment of surrender that the church has one of its greatest responsibilities. A new child has now been birthed into the kingdom and awaits love, nurturing, care, fathering, mentoring, and training, which simply equates to discipling, a term that has become increasingly harder to define and execute.

Due to the nature of the modern church there is a need for people to serve in a variety of ways. I have heard the phrase many times that a happy Christian is a busy Christian, and we use the examples from scripture that a life following Jesus is a life of serving. While these elements are true no doubt, they have been used to manipulate believers into serving for the wrong reasons and have therefore created a culture of shallow and weak servants that experience the famed "burnout". We have all seen good people experience burnout from serving the Lord and yet the Lord says that His burden is light and His yoke is easy. If the Lord's burden and yoke is so light and easy, why are so many good people serving in church so weary and tired, needing to take extended breaks from ministry just to refresh and recoup. This doesn't make sense when the load is easy and light that there are such a high number of "resting" people in our churches. Is it possible that we the church have traded the burden of Jesus, which is light and easy, for the burden of man which is heavy and difficult. There are many different reasons that people don't serve in ministries inside or outside the church with lack of time being at the top of the list. As we move people into greater knowledge of Jesus's light and easy burden, they will realize that they can't live without serving and volunteering is the path to a fulfilling and purposeful life.

My dad used to tell me that, "You will do what you want to do". This simply meant that I would make time for what I felt was important to me, and would spend time with things that I placed a value on as beneficial to my life. Therein lies the key to building your ministry teams to serve your church and the visitor. Jesus was all about the individual and many stories of Jesus dealt specifically and uniquely around one particular person and their needs. It was almost as though he operated His ministry to draw people into relationship with God by building them up and helping them find the freedom they lacked. As a result of this type of approach they served Him with devotion and faithfulness. People want to be a part of something that builds them, not drains them. They don't want to give everything they have physically, emotionally, and spiritually with nothing in return. I have heard many people encourage people to serve as a sacrifice and that they will one day receive their reward. Though our life to Christ is certainly a sacrifice of the flesh and one day we will most assuredly receive a reward for our efforts, this is difficult for many to swallow and teeters on the motivation versus manipulation fence. It is better if we cultivate a culture of a fulfillment of purpose rather than a culture of turnover and burnout. Burnout happens when you give out more than you take in. What you take in fills your tank and what you give out empties your tank.

I recently had a precious brother in the Lord ask me how to avoid burnout. I asked him to define first in his life the things that bring refreshment to him. I told him to list out all the items that would fill his tank. I then suggested that he make sure that he does those things on a consistent basis so that his tank never becomes empty. Too many times precious servants of the Lord have given all they have in the tank, and as a car can only go so far on a tank of gas, we too can only go so far before we need to fill up again. We have all seen too many good people out of gas on the side of the road, now needing help to fill their tanks. It's a tragedy of the highest kind in the church and to keep people on a path of fulfillment of purpose you will need to establish a culture that allows people to keep their tank full. A car that continually has fuel in the tank is easy to drive, but a car that constantly runs out of gas along the side of the road creates a load too tough to bear. So when you are establishing and recruiting for your ministry team, design your teams to not only provide an opportunity for people to give from their tank, but also replenish it as well.

For years the concept of using people to build ministries has not settled well within my spirit. It just seemed wrong to think about using people to build ministries, though looking through the eyes of religious church tradition it made perfect sense to get people volunteering as fast as we can because the church cannot operate without volunteers. We the church didn't have to provide any incentives or rewards because the scriptures said that you would have a reward when you go to heaven for your serving. It was not our responsibility to create a fun and uplifting serving experience, but just provide an opportunity for sacrifice, and one day God will repay your service according to His generosity. The problem with this is it doesn't work, but only fosters a turnover and burnout culture among the churches. People get tired and weary of serving, and even the best, top choice people fall prey to an empty tank on the side of the road. If we really love our people then we will not use them to build ministries, but on the contrary will use our ministries to build the people.

We have to shift the way we think, a cognitive adjustment in how we view each other and the precious believers that fill our sanctuaries. We can no longer afford to accept casualties along the roadside with empty gas tanks. We have to care for the flock better and be the example of Jesus that He intended for us to be. We all must strive to figure out the changes that need to be made within our ministry teams in order to use them to build the volunteers serving in them, and not just be a vacuum that sucks dry all the good within. The church can no longer be an example that changes volunteers like we change light bulbs and just replace them when they burnout. The kingdom of God is at stake and the lives of those that serve are hanging in the balance. Too much damage has already been done, by using people to build ministries. Jesus didn't die for ministries; He died for people.

You will need to ask, "How can this ministry not only serve the vision of the church, but also build and serve the volunteers that serve in it?" We have to add the second part of that statement and not just stop at how this ministry can serve the vision of the church. Every ministry team no matter how small or large can function to grow and build those that serve in it, while simultaneously fulfilling the vision of the church. In reality ministry teams like ushering and greeters should fulfill a two-fold purpose; to serve those that walk through the doors of the church and build up those that are serving within the team. Most of the time we only have a plan for serving those that walk through the doors of the church. For the health of the church and the health of those that serve, it will be critical for a shift to take place in the hearts of our pastoral staff, ministry staff, and lay leadership.

The ministry team that focuses not only on serving the congregants and community but also has built in mechanisms and strategies for building the team members themselves will never be in want of volunteers. This type of ministry team is called a "Transformational Ministry Team". A transformational ministry team transforms all who are involved with the team, whether it is from receiving from the team or serving on the team. All parties involved become transformed, fulfilled, and drawn into fellowship and relationship with the Lord. We will need to make a move from just ministry teams to transformational ministry teams, if we really want to make an impact in the lives of those we serve and serve with.

Another thing about transformational ministry teams is that they are attractive. There is nothing worse than being recruited for a team that is "needy". A needy team just screams losing, and no one wants to be part of a losing team. You will go to extremes when your team becomes needy, like stooping to beg from the pulpit for help or other non-attractive methods of recruitment. Attractive ministry teams draw you in and entice you to want to know more and usually there is an abundance of volunteers where everyone seems to be light and easy versus heavy and burdensome. We all want to be around people that exude the light and easy, but rarely do we want to be around people that always seem to be heavy and burdensome. Transformational ministry teams that build people create an attractive atmosphere that people want to be a part of.

You can't help but have people at the center of your heart when building transformational ministry teams. These teams care about the people involved not just the tasks that need to be accomplished. When interviewing people to serve on a ministry team it's always good to find out about them, and what God is doing in their life. We coach our team leaders not to just recruit for their team, but to recruit for all of the teams. This is to ensure that we care about the people more than we care about filling a hole on our team. It's the difference between motivating volunteers to serve and manipulating volunteers to serve. There is a really fine line here between motivating and manipulating, so much so that we often cross it without even knowing it. It's a subtle line that actually we have been very comfortable crossing for years. Let me give you an example. Have you ever said the words to a potential volunteer, "You know, you would be great at greeting", or, "You would be a great usher", when you don't even really know the person. I have had pastors tell me that they or their team will do this to first time visitors, and then boast that that's how they get their volunteers. I am amazed at how you can know nothing about the person, their heart, past experiences, what God is currently doing in their life, and boldly tell them how great they would be at doing something. You don't even know the person and you are telling them how great they are just to get them on your team. Usually this happens from team leaders or pastors that are trying to fill holes in the ministry teams. When you recruit people for the purpose of them serving the team, or filling a hole in the team and not for the purpose of building and serving their life's purpose you have manipulated them into serving. It doesn't sound like manipulating when you are being sweet and telling them how great they would be at doing something, but the motive is wrong since you are recruiting them to serve for what you can get out of them, meeting your need, instead of what you can deposit in them, meeting their needs. See, if we use people to build ministries than we only care about the ministries and the people become just a tool and a resource to accomplish the ministry. We can't forget that the ministry "is" the people. It just doesn't make any sense to tear down and wear out people so that we can minister to people. We will burnout our volunteer people in order to build up and serve the people walking through our front doors. We tear down one person so we can build up another.

Even in the workplace there needs to be a sense of fulfillment for employees otherwise they too will fizzle in their excitement and succumb to the doldrums of the 8:00 to 5:00 monotony. Pfizer & Company is known for having the happiest employees and ranking with the top companies in employee satisfaction. The rating is based on different factors but one of those factors is the degree of dedication to providing employees with the tools and resources needed to succeed in their careers. This principle reiterates that you can successfully complete your company vision, which for them as one of the largest biopharmaceutical companies in the world, discovers, develops, manufactures, and sells healthcare products worldwide. They are not only able to successfully provide healthcare products to the public, but also able to supply what is needed for health to their employees lives and careers. We too, the church can provide what is needed for the health of our volunteers to stay healthy and avoid the dreaded burnout. I like how one of our team leaders, Jennifer Spriuell puts it, when she says your not losing a volunteer, you're losing a whole component of God. People are not just volunteers. They make up a whole component of God that breathes life into your visitors, regular attenders, members, and staff.

If you need volunteers for your ministry teams then it's time to get to know more people. Find people you don't know in the church and get to know them. Ask them a few questions first so that you can get to know them better. Once you know them and have a sense of what God is doing in their life it is easier for you to suggest areas of ministry that may fit their goals or passions, or at least get them started toward knowing their purpose. One of the first questions you could ask a potential volunteer is, "What moves you emotionally?" This really is a passion question to get to know what they are passionate about. I want to know what things spark people, what things they would want changed in life if they could change it. It reveals to you the things that they become emotionally charged about, like homelessness, feeding the hungry, politics, children, teens, abortion, etc... A second question is similar to this and basically asks the question, "If you had unlimited money, staff, and resources at you disposal and knew you couldn't fail, what would you do with your life?" These two questions will quickly give you the insight into their heart of what God may want to do with them, and allows you to see the real them without the limitations of budget, people, and resources, which most hide behind.

In addition to passion assessments you can also use DISC profile assessments, Spiritual Gifts tests, and S.H.A.P.E profiles, to determine the gifts and strengths of each potential volunteer. This helps you, and them, know more about how God has fashioned and designed them to be a blessing to the body of Christ and to the community. As you can imagine there are things you don't want to do while recruiting volunteers. Your ministry team is fulfilling multiple ministry purposes and as you recruit you are enlisting people to not only fulfill a ministry function for the body of Christ, but also helping them enlist into their ministry and fulfilling their ministry purpose. Here are seven things you don't want to do while recruiting that may help you out.

7 Things your team leaders don't want to do while recruiting volunteers

1. Don't recruit for yourself or for your own ministry team.

This is difficult to do with so many needs in our teams, but this will keep you from recruiting people into your team for your purposes. Instead it is better to recruit with the person in mind instead of your team in mind. Help them connect with a ministry team that best suits them, versus just plugging them into a team with the biggest holes.

2. Don't force or beg people to get involved **(family members or close friends)**.

More times than not, when you recruit family members or close friends you are just plugging them into a hole on the team. Each person has a unique gifting, calling, and strengths. If you really find out what those strengths are, you may find that they may be best suited for a ministry team other than the one their family member is on. This will also ensure longevity for the person and stability for the team since fitting strengths with ministry teams provides more fulfillment that just serving in a ministry team without intentionality.

3. Don't look down on those that don't want to be involved.

We need to foster an environment of excitement not criticism, attraction and not condemnation, and though someone may not want to serve when you ask them, it doesn't mean they don't want to serve. They may just need the right coaching to help them find an area where they fit the best and the ministry that brings the most fulfillment to their life and passion.

4. Don't tell people they would be good at something when you don't really know them.

We talked about this earlier in this chapter but bears to say again. This steers people in wrong direction and thus causes disappointment and delusion with the team member. Creating an environment that shows you really care about the person and what God is doing and wants to do in their life will go a long way in them accomplishing all that God has for them. Just telling them that they would be good at a ministry position when you don't know them is really just driving them to serve your purposes and gain, instead of directing them in a ministry position that would motivate them to serve for God's purposes and gain.

5. Don't promise leadership roles.

Promising leadership or other promotions just to get volunteers to serve leads to disappointment and frustration. Leadership is developed over time and promising something you can't deliver will only cause you, your team, and your church to lose respect and credibility.

6. Don't talk down or belittle other ministry teams or team leaders.

This undermines authority and creates dissention and strife in the body of Christ. Highlighting a ministry team as better than the other or warning a potential volunteer about a bad leader in order to steer them in a different direction will create animosity in your leadership and disunity among the ministry teams.

7. Don't offer occasional monetary benefits or other perks.

Don't offer cash payouts to volunteers or other perks to try and entice someone to serve on your team. If your team has a hiring model like many nursery ministries do, then that person is an employee or paid staff member, but offering the occasional monetary benefit for volunteering will set your ministry team up for failure and a price you should not be willing to pay.

It's an amazing responsibility for the care and nurturing of those that have decided to follow Jesus and to serve Him in the kingdom. The work of the great commission of making disciples and raising up the body of Christ to impact communities, states, and countries, requires a tremendous amount of effort and strategy. Though we don't see a lot of instruction about ministry teams from a scriptural standpoint our modern society dictates the use of them for the gospel proclamation and the development of the believers. Whether or not Solomon had employees, servants, slaves, or volunteers, the use of his teams sets the standard on what can be accomplished through the appropriate use of them. If Solomon can use his teams to change the life of a visitor than we too can use our teams to change the life of our visitors, not only fulfilling the vision of the ministry but also bringing a full and purposeful life to those that serve so faithfully on them.

Good things always start with good ingredients! Training of your church's volunteer teams and leadership is an impartation not an orientation.

CHAPTER EIGHT

RAISING UP LEADERSHIP

YOU NEED LEADERS

Listen now to my voice; I will give you counsel, and God will be with you: Stand before God for the people, so that you may bring the difficulties to God. And you shall teach them the statutes and the laws, and show them the way in which they must walk and the work they must do. Moreover you shall select from all the people able men, such as fear God, men of truth, hating covetousness; and place such over them to be rulers of thousands, rulers of hundreds, rulers of fifties, and rulers of tens, Exodus 18:20-21. Moses, in this passage is receiving instruction on how to care, develop, and mature the people from his father in law, Jethro. He was told to raise up leaders and to give them responsibilities to minister and care for the people. Previously, Moses had been trying to accomplish all the work of caring for the people himself and was failing miserably, wearing out both him and the people.

The institutionalized church over the years has fostered a mentality that the pastor is required to do all the work and the people are to come and receive from all the wisdom and understanding that he possesses. It has essentially created a silo effect that keeps leadership potential and maturity among the people suppressed. Jethro tells Moses to "show them the way" in which they must walk and the work they must do. Verse 22 and 23 of Exodus 18 reveals the result and reward of this "showing" by saying that it will be easier for Moses, since the leaders he raises up will help him bear the burden making the overall load lighter so that he can endure, and the people will be blessed since they will get their needs met faster and will be able to go to their places in peace.

YOU NEED TO CHOOSE GOOD LEADERS

The first thing Moses was required to do was raise up leaders that were able men, such as fear God, men of truth, and hating covetousness. There were criteria that needed to be met by these potential leaders for them to serve and lead over the people. Too many times in our churches, especially new church plants, we tend to find warm bodies that are breathing and ask them to lead a ministry team or oversee a portion of our services. The most difficult thing about this method is usually it is very hard to remove someone from a position once you have entrusted them with it. The reason Moses was given criteria for leadership is that it ensures and raises the quality of care provided to the people. The godly quality and character of the men would ensure the highest quality of care for the people they served. God using Jethro to speak to Moses, was revealing to Moses how important the people were and how deep His love for them was. God wanted to make sure that the people were taken care of with the utmost integrity and with the best quality possible. Moses did not choose anyone that was just faithful, and though maybe implied, faithfulness was not even listed as part of the criteria, and yet faithfulness ranks at the top of the list for leadership roles for many of today's churches. There were more requirements than just being faithful for the potential leaders to possess. Each potential leader had to possess the right ingredients. Good things always start with good ingredients! Have you ever thought about what a good system with bad ingredients would produce? Or what about a bad system with good ingredients?

Have you, your spouse, or have you known someone that has cooked something with inferior ingredients? I am sure the outcome was not the intended desire. Top chefs know that the only way to produce a quality product is to begin with quality ingredients. The ingredients, which are not created by the chef, are brought together for a common purpose to produce something that will serve and benefit others. The higher quality the ingredients, the higher benefit the product will be to those that partake of it.

In a chef's search for high quality ingredients they will be looking for ingredients that are not defected, diseased, filled with pollutants, decayed, toxic, stale, diluted, or out of season. In choosing our leaders we too should be looking for leaders that are not, in a spiritual sense, decayed, diseased, filled with worldly pollutants, or spiritually diluted. No one is perfect, even the men that were serving with Moses were not perfect, but they did meet a certain standard set forth by the Lord in order to lead with the highest quality possible. One of the first ingredients Moses had to look for was whether or not the men were "able men". This one ingredient has always baffled me since we have so much eternally riding on our ministries. We work for the creator of the universe and have such a high stake with precious lives on the line, and yet we come up short often when it comes to choosing wisely, who we entrust with leadership roles in order to provide the greatest impact possible.

I like watching NFL football and have often thought about what kind of league the NFL would be if they built their teams and leadership like the church did. The NFL build their teams for the absolute greatest impact possible, mostly on Sunday. It's an impact that will bring them the coveted Lombardi Trophy at the end of a successful winning season. The NFL franchises spend an enormous amount of time and effort into their recruiting for their teams to the point that it's almost mind-boggling. They have built statistic sheets on all of their positions and potential candidates to determine if the candidate is the right fit for the position. A tremendous amount of detail and strategy goes into every position, player, coach, admin, and marketing, and the real purpose for all of this effort is to create a sustainable bottom line that produces money and a trophy at the end of the year. Is money more important than the Gospel message? Is a trophy more important than our unbelieving visitor coming into relationship with Jesus? It's a little scary to think that the NFL will spend more time and effort to protect a cash producing bottom line, than we the church would to reach our communities with the greatest message known to mankind. 100 years from now no one is going to care about who won the SuperBowl or what the salary caps were for the NFL. So instead of the NFL using the church's methods to build their teams, maybe we should take a play from their playbook, establish a well thought out strategy, define the elusive details, and put in the effort that they do, not to produce a temporary monetary impact, but to produce an eternal kingdom impact.

As Moses began to look for men that were "able" and possessed leadership potential we too should have a strategy to constantly be looking for "able" people and those that possess leadership qualities. There will be a big difference in your results when you choose people that are able and can faithfully fulfill the leadership role you assign them. There are certain leadership qualities that stand out that can prove beneficial to your search if you know what to look for. Below is a list of leadership qualities you can use when choosing leaders for your team, and a comparison of worker qualities to help you know the difference. In trying to identify the good ingredients in people for leadership roles you will want to consider these leadership characteristics. You could use this list in conjunction with the flow chart boxes from chapter 6 to lay out a leadership structure for your church or organization. All of your volunteer and staff positions will be filled with either a leader or a worker. Leaders are not better than workers and workers and not better than leaders, but each one fills a valuable role for your church, organization, or business.

Leaders vs. Workers

1. A leader is people focused, whereas a worker is task focused.

2. A leader equips others to get the job done, whereas a worker gets the job done.

3. A leader creates vision, whereas the worker just works the vision.

4. A leader inspires others to produce results, whereas the worker produces results.

5. A leader solves problems and offers solutions, whereas the worker reports problems.

6. A leader understands all roles, whereas a worker understands their role.

7. A leader can train others to do, whereas a worker likes to do it better themself.

8. A leader helps others set and achieve their goals, whereas a worker has their goals set for them.

9. A leader develops, whereas a worker maintains what has been developed.

10. A leader thinks outside the box, whereas a worker stays comfortably inside the box.

11. A leader motivates and inspires, whereas a worker is better with motivation and inspiration.

12. A leader questions what and why we do things, whereas a worker questions how and when we do things.

13. A leader is responsible for others, whereas a worker is responsible for themself.

14. A leader can speak publicly to a group, whereas a worker shies away from public speaking.

15. A leader creates an environment for change, whereas a worker maintains control and order.

16. A leader leads people, whereas a worker works the work.

17. A leader does the right thing, whereas a worker does things right.

18. A leader is outcome oriented, whereas a worker is rules oriented.

YOU NEED TO MENTOR YOUR LEADERS

Upon Moses choosing his leaders he was now to teach them the statutes and the laws, and show them the way in which they must walk and the work they must do. Moses didn't just choose the leaders and then say, "off you go", for them to try and figure out how to lead and care for the people. God gave Moses a command to teach them and to show them the way they must walk and the work they must do. There was a teaching and a showing that would now need to be implemented. The choosing of the leadership was only the beginning, and now must be followed up with a life of training that incorporated teaching and showing.

We have all heard, and probably have been apart of the sink or swim teaching method. My mother recently told me a story about how she learned to swim when she was young. She was swinging over water on a rope when she plunged into the water. When she hit the water her raft around her body went straight up as she went straight down. A quick sense of anxiety set in, since no one was around to help her, and then a bout of intense paddling began. My dad was just thrown in the water by his uncle when he was young. They both survived the lesson, but the experience provided is not recommended. No one really likes the sink or swim methodology when it comes to trying to learn how to do something. This method is famous for causing two elements to rise in the human body. Stress is one of those elements and the other is a vow to never get put in that position again. It is absolutely the worst way of training someone for a position, role, or task. We see a great example of mentorship in the bible through the life of Jesus and his disciples. The disciples spent three years walking with Jesus and discussing kingdom principles and how to affectively minister to those around them, discussing victories and failures that they experienced. Out of all the pedagogic systems available none is used more than the lecture, and through hundreds of studies on the subject none have been found to be less effective. People don't want to be talked to, they want to be engaged and involved. They want to feel like they are a vital part of the overall impact, and there is no better feeling than feeling like you are trained for what you are called to do. Here are 8 thoughts about a team that has been trained.

- A trained team creates a secure environment.
- A trained team moves the organization forward.
- A trained team is productive.
- A trained team reduces confusion.
- A trained team has a sense of accomplishment.
- A trained team cares for the people.
- A trained team is a support to the pastor.
- A trained team honors God.

There is a familiar 5 step mentoring process that I first read about in John Maxwell's book, "Developing The Leaders Around You", that is often quoted but rarely implemented. The steps are:

1. I do, you watch.
2. I do, you help.
3. You do, I help.
4. You do, I watch.
5. You do, someone else watches.

What I like about this mentoring model is that an impartation is taking place during the mentoring. Training of your church's volunteer teams and leadership is an impartation not an orientation. Orientations are meetings to get you oriented on how to do something, or tells you about something, but it misses the mark relationally of why you do it, and the value of your doing it. When you impart your DNA or your culture into those that are serving for you and with you, you will be creating an intentional force of purpose. This allows everyone to move to the beat of the same drum, moving the organization forward and allowing for all team members to have an understanding of who you are and why you do what you do. Looking back at King Solomon and the visiting queen of Sheba, Solomon no doubt imparted his heart and DNA to his servants, those that worked on his house, those that prepared the food for his table, the servants, cupbearers, and his waiters. His impartation of his heart was so strong that an unbelieving queen, who traveled great distances, not only heard godly wisdom from the king's mouth, but also saw godly wisdom by the way she was served by his servants. What Solomon was able to speak out of his mouth, the queen was able to see through his servant teams. It's when you look out in your church and see that your ministry teams are fulfilling the vision of the house that a peace fills the inner most part of your being. To know that all that is in your heart as a leader is being visually expressed in those you lead is one of the greatest rewards a leader can receive.

YOU NEED TO IMPART YOUR CULTURE

When a healthy impartation of the vision, or of your heart takes place among your leadership and ministry teams, a fruitful culture begins to emerge. Every church organization has a culture whether it's the culture you desire or not. The challenge is to establish the culture that fulfills the vision of your church not a culture that works against the vision.

You see this sabotaging culture in the business world quite frequently when a new hire has been brought in from outside the organization. Let's use colors for an example of culture. Company X has a culture of "blue", and they have systems and processes in place to make sure that everyone employed understands and becomes part of the blue culture. Over time the systems, processes, top level leadership have done a great job, and looking down on the company from a birds eye view they have succeeded in becoming a blue culture. One day, they lose one of their executive leadership team, and unfortunately had not trained/mentored properly a replacement from within the blue organization, and now are forced to hire from the outside. Obviously, this outside new hire who comes from a different color culture, like red for example, does not have the blue culture instilled in them and will need to be mentored in blue. Some have said that it takes an average of 3 years to establish culture. If that is true than it will take 3 years for this new hire to turn from red to blue, affecting everyone they lead with the remnants of red that was instilled in him from his other company.

The reason I bring this up is because in raising up leadership it is better to hire from within your organization, since you have had time to establish your culture and DNA into your leaders, and therefore don't lose progress in moving the ministry or organization forward. To successfully do this you will need to include as a part of your culture a "no holes" mentality or simply a master succession plan. A no holes mentality is when you look at your organizational chart and you have identified a replacement for every position, from the top pastoral position all the way down to the volunteer positions. Every position has a successor and that successor is currently trained not only in their current position, but also as much as possible, in the position that may be required of them in the future. One of the qualities of a leader is that they are able to produce more leaders that will in turn produce more leaders.

In the example of Company X above the failure of that leader to duplicate themselves to someone within the company creates a delay in productivity. Where we may not be concerned about the delay in productivity for Company X, since dollars is their focus, we should however, be greatly concerned about the productivity of our churches, where eternal lives are the focus. When large businesses have to reestablish culture among their employees it can cost millions of dollars in lost progress. When the church has to reestablish culture among its volunteers, leaders, or staff it can cost something more valuable than dollars. It cost the church time and the time lost equates to salvations, marriages restored, disciples made, addictions healed, communities affected, and ultimately a world reached.

WE CAN DO IT

For me, I look at Solomon and admire the heart of excellence, the pursuit of wisdom, and the fervency that he possessed for daily life and for leadership. The inspirational example of his ministry teams being able to show wisdom visually, and the effect that this display of serving had on a skeptical, unbelieving, first time visitor is truly remarkable.

We really don't have any idea of the impact on the community that our ministry teams can have. We will have to fight the raging current of skepticism that will speak loudly that people aren't really impacted by the greeters or our usher teams, and only make returning decisions based on the music and the preaching. We will have to fight a lackadaisical spiritual culture that minimizes the value of church volunteers to those that just serve the church's purpose and not the main purpose of reaching our communities.

The church has been the greatest tool for evangelizing the modern world. God is working feverously every day to create circumstances and situations that will bring people to church to hear about Him. God is our greatest advocate in entrusting us with the precious lives of those that live in our neighborhoods, our city, state, country, and ultimately the world. If God is working so hard to bring people to church, so that they may be drawn into fellowship with him, we should work just as hard to receive those that He brings us. We must have an urgency that brings us to asking the hard questions about how we reach our communities for God. It's in these moments that I believe God will provide and has provided solutions.

With the lack of excellence and the embracing of minimalism in our society God has given us an amazing opportunity to stand out and attract a hurting world to Him. A combined effort among the ministry teams of your church has the ability to create a catalytic change. Our world is in a desperate peril of neglect of love and care. You don't have to go too far to find your neighbor hurting or even church folks spiritually wounded. We will have to reconcile the balance of what we are praying for and what we are preparing for. God will not give us what we are praying for, if we are not faithful to prepare for it. He cares too much for people to entrust them to a church or organization that will not prepare to care for them. Remember, the horse is prepared for the battle, but victory belongs to the Lord. God will bring us victory in our communities but we must prepare for it, and the greatest place to prepare for the community is with your ministry teams. If God can help Solomon impart his DNA of wisdom and excellence into those that served on his teams to affect those that came for a visit, I have full confidence that God will help us too. He will help us, and provide the wisdom needed in building our ministry teams in such a way that will bring about His glory to a hurting world, and provide an oasis of love and hope to the visitor, and those in need.

About the Author

Lee West is an Executive Pastor for Liberty Church, based out of Pensacola, Florida. He regularly works with ministry teams within the local church to inspire, motivate, and encourage excellence in order to see churches grow, capture more salvations, and create an impact on their communities. Lee has owned several businesses, served in corporate sales and marketing roles, served in pastoral roles including involvement in overseas missions in Russia, Mexico, Bahamas, India, Ukraine, and the Philippines. He holds a B.A in Pastoral Ministries from Liberty Bible College and an M.ED in Educational Administration from Oral Roberts University.

He resides with his lovely wife Missy in the beautiful Gulf Coast area of Gulf Shores, Alabama.

For Additional Information Contact

Lee West

info@readthevisitor.com

www.ReadTheVisitor.com

www.LeeWest.org

Bush Publishing

www.BushPublishing.com